STORIES FROM THE

MOHAWK VALLEY

STORIES FROM THE MOHAWK VALLEY

The Painted Rocks, the Good Benedict Arnold & More

BOB CUDMORE

THE History PRESS

Published by The History Press
Charleston, SC 29403
www.historypress.net

Front cover, top: World War I bond drive in downtown Amsterdam. *Montgomery County Department of History and Archives. Bottom*: Rufus Grider's depiction of the Painted Rocks in Amsterdam, painted in 1887. *New York State Archives*.

Back cover: Portrait of Sir William Johnson. *Montgomery County Department of History and Archives*; *Winter in the Valley of the Mohawks*, painting by Len Tantillo. *Courtesy of the artist.*

First published 2011

Manufactured in the United States

ISBN 978.1.60949.058.4

Library of Congress Cataloging-in-Publication Data

Cudmore, Bob, 1945-
Stories from the Mohawk Valley : the Painted Rocks, the good Benedict Arnold and more / Bob Cudmore.
p. cm.
Includes bibliographical references.
ISBN 978-1-60949-058-4
1. Mohawk River Valley (N.Y.)--History--Anecdotes. 2. Mohawk River Valley (N.Y.)--History, Local--Anecdotes. 3. Mohawk River Valley (N.Y.)--Biography--Anecdotes. I. Title.
F127.M55C84 2011
974.7'6--dc23
2011026792

To Audrey Sears, for her love and her love of stories

Contents

Foreword, by R.H. von Hasseln 9
Preface and Acknowledgements 11

Old Days
An Ancient Story 13
The Valley of the Kanyenkehaka 16
The Painted Rocks 19
Sir William Johnson and Slavery 21
Did George Washington Sit Here? 24
Albert Vedder and Joseph Hagaman 26

The Way West
Port Jackson on the Erie Canal 29
Amsterdam's Benedict Arnold 32
Green Hill 33
Amsterdam and Its Railroads 33
The Fonda, Johnstown & Gloversville Railroad 37

The Mills
The Sanfords of Amsterdam 41
The Looms of Mohawk 47
Underwear, Buttons and Strikes 53
Rug City Was also Broom City 55

Contents

The Family that Built Amsterdam 58
Deindustrialization, the End of an Era 61
Urban Renewal 64

The People of the Valley
Amsterdam's Psychedelic Philosopher 67
Queen Libby of Fonda 70
African American History 72
Fritz Vogt—Homeless Man Who Chronicled Home Life 75
Kirk Douglas 77
Singer Arlene Fontana 80
The Daiquiris 83
Artist Mary Van der Veer 85
The Camacho Family 88
Mary—An Immigrant's Story 90
Three Memorable Mayors of Amsterdam 94
Michael Wytrwal—The Polish Mayor of Amsterdam 100
More than a Waitress 103
Keep Cool at Duchessi's 105
The DiMezza Bank 109
Officer Nelson—Big, Gruff but Nice 111

The Wars and the Warriors
Civil War 113
Amsterdam's Armory 117
The Roughneck and the Cook 119
Guadalcanal Diary 122
Townsends, Watroba, Haas 123
Honor Roll 126
USS *Amsterdam* 128

The Museum and the Library
Walter Elwood and His Museum 133
Amsterdam Free Library 136

Further Reading on Mohawk Valley History 139
About the Author 143

Foreword

The Voice of the Mohawk Valley

Kirk Douglas may be Amsterdam's favorite son, but Bob Cudmore is probably its most generally admired.

There was always enough Amsterdam twang in Kirk Douglas's voice to make me wonder if I should claim that Spartacus or Vincent van Gogh were Amsterdamians, but Bob Cudmore's voice is the one most people think of as the "Voice of the Mohawk Valley." Whether it is the daily radio programs or the weekly newspaper columns, people hereabouts think that if Bob talked about it, it's not only true but it's also important.

They're right, and it's more to do with the way Bob tells them than that they love being told about themselves. Personally, as a local historian, I have been grateful to him (and sometimes a little jealous) for getting these stories on the air and into print. I've told Bob that he's done as much to chronicle the Lower Mohawk Valley as many of its most prominent historians. He won't have any of that; he's just "telling its stories."

But for other readers, it's not just his devotion to the content but also the humanity that underlies it. He gets what these stories *really* mean—that keeps readers coming back for more, and not just the hometown fans.

I've wondered about this nonresident interest in his articles on the local area for a while, so recently I sat down to talk about this with one of the foremost experts on the region: Bob Cudmore. We agreed that despite many changes, Amsterdam remains a very special place. Close to everything—yet from any direction, you still have to drive through the woods to see it arise from the valley. It's a true microcosm, and on that small stage plays out love and hate, triumph and tragedy, violence and compassion, pettiness and greatness—all the larger for their tighter focus.

And that's when I realized why I had been reading his articles long before I moved here. Bob's stories capture universal qualities, and because they do, anyone can see something of his or her own hometown experiences in them.

And there is something else special about Amsterdam, which we didn't discuss that day. I now live less than a mile in either direction from the two respective homes where Bob Cudmore and Kirk Douglas grew up. As I move about the same streets, I can sense the ebb and flow—the noisy but fascinating parade of many different people interacting in one small area as they build new lives for themselves—that these two must have also felt only a generation or so apart. I would never compare my skills to theirs, but I think I can understand what underlies and informs their common desire to tell important stories, and tell them well, though in very different ways. Amsterdam inspires great storytellers.

Many of the stories in this book are expanded from Bob's *Daily Gazette* column. It's the first thing I read each Saturday over my morning coffee, scissors and paste at the ready to add the information to the city's historical files. I've acquired so many clippings that sometimes I've wished there were some way to suspend Bob over the file cabinet and simply shake the stories out of him directly into the proper folders.

But now I may not have to.

After you've enjoyed these stories, tell your friends and family or give them a copy as a gift; if enough copies sell, then maybe Bob will have to do a second and third volume. And then I can put up the scissors, clean the paste off my coffee cup and just enjoy them like everyone else, resident or not.

R.H. von Hasseln
City Historian
Amsterdam, New York
July 2011

Preface and Acknowledgements

Have you heard about the Painted Rocks on the Mohawk River? Did you know that the 115th Civil War regiment raised in Fonda spent part of the war in Union custody? What do you make of Amsterdam's Benjamin Paul Blood, who got a psychedelic circle going among early twentieth-century philosophers? There are stories everywhere in the Mohawk Valley.

Polish leader Michael Wytrwal loved "welfare" peanut butter. The aptly named Queen Libby stopped a train in Fonda. When Ralph Camacho came to Amsterdam from Puerto Rico, a man could lose one job at night and have a new one the next morning.

A good Benedict Arnold is buried in one of our cemeteries. George Washington could have used the privy at Old Fort Johnson—and the restored facility is still there. Amsterdam produced two Kentucky Derby winners.

The Amsterdam area, where many of these stories take place, is set apart from the urban sprawl of Albany, Schenectady and Troy. Amsterdam's main industry for many years was carpet making—quite an artistic product.

We are feisty and colorful—good company for the most part, if more than a little nostalgic for the old days. It's no accident that bestselling novelist Richard Russo came from our neck of the woods. Or that Amsterdam's best-known former resident became an actor: Kirk Douglas.

As local native Mike Van Allen put it on Facebook, "I think one of the best things about growing up in Amsterdam was that it prepared you for life outside of Amsterdam. As kids, I believe we weren't sheltered. We saw bookies. We knew about guys selling stuff out of their trunks. We had seen great parades. We had friends of every race, religion and ethnic background."

Many tales are told in this volume, and I hope you enjoy them. Many stories have been left out, giving rise to the idea that this volume may have a sequel.

And do me a favor—don't pass the book around. Recommend it, by all means. But encourage your relatives and friends to buy their own copies. We have printed enough to go around. If you see me, I have a few in my trunk.

Acknowledgements

Audrey Sears provided immeasurable help as this book was being written, posing many questions that hadn't occurred to me. Thanks to Irving Dean, of the *Daily Gazette*, who has edited my history columns. Gerald B. Snyder was the go-to photo guy. Amsterdam city historian Robert von Hasseln was most helpful, as were Montgomery County historian Kelly Farquhar, Fulton County historian Peter Betz, former Montgomery County historian Jacqueline Murphy and Ann Peconie of the Walter Elwood Museum. The late *Recorder* columnist and historian Hugh P. Donlon is frequently quoted in these pages. Many of the stories benefit from research done with Steve Dunn in producing our documentary about Amsterdam. My children and their significant others—Bob Cudmore Jr. and Tamar Sarnoff and Kathleen Cudmore Bokan and her husband, Mike—humor their father in his projects and are dear to my heart.

My wife, Mary; parents, Clarence and Julia; sister Arlene; and aunt Vera Cudmore did not live to see this book published. Please enjoy it on their behalf.

Old Days

An Ancient Story

Archaeologists from the Louis Berger Group unearthed hundreds of historic artifacts on the north shore of the Mohawk River in Amsterdam in the general area of the mouth of the North Chuctanunda Creek in 2010. The dig was named the Chuctanunda Terrace Site. The artifacts include spearheads and arrowheads that are estimated to be between five hundred and five thousand years old. The artifacts were found undisturbed and in chronological layers. The oldest items were on the bottom, the newer ones closer to the top.

Eight of the oldest objects found are displayed in one photograph. Delland M. Gould, senior field supervisor for the Louis Berger Group (LBG), said these are projectile points that would have been attached to wooden darts or spears for hunting. The small projectile point at the far left of the top row is the oldest—estimated to date from five thousand years ago. It is similar to projectile points found at the Brewerton Corner archaeological site in Central New York. If the date estimate is correct, the people who used this projectile point were alive at about the same time as the Egyptians were building their first pyramid.

Gould said it is not known who the people were who lived in the area five thousand years ago. It is estimated that humans first crossed into North America from Asia some thirteen to fourteen thousand years ago, possibly earlier.

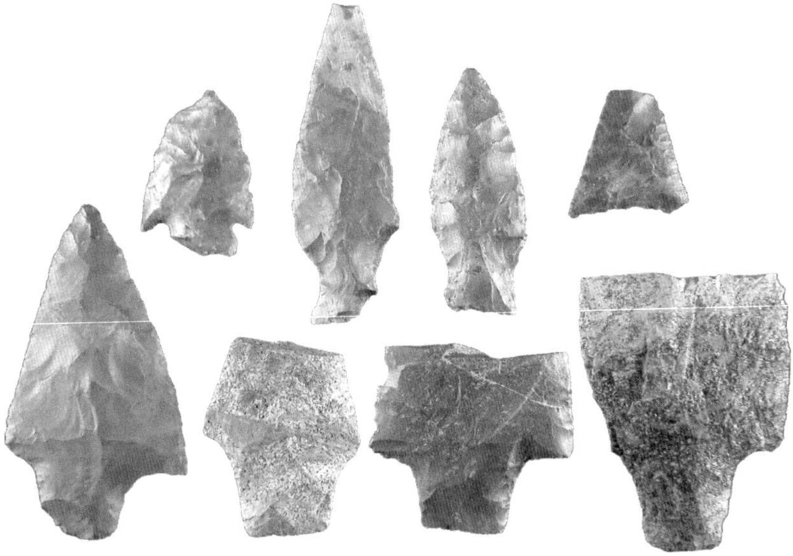

Projectile points unearthed in an archaeological dig in Amsterdam are from five hundred to five thousand years old. *The Louis Berger Group.*

Relatively speaking, the seven other projectile points in the picture are much newer. To the right of the Brewerton Corners object in the top row are two fishtail points estimated to be twenty-eight hundred to three thousand years old.

The triangle-shaped point at the upper far right is believed to be a remnant of the Mohawk culture from five hundred years ago, before the encounter with the first European settlers. It is possible that this point was an arrowhead. The bow and arrow were developed in North America about fifteen hundred years ago. The four projectile points in the bottom row are estimated to be thirty-five hundred years old.

Most of the projectile points were fashioned from a kind of stone called chert, not found in the immediate area of the Amsterdam dig. Gould said the nearest source of chert was upriver near Randall and Yosts at the Noses, where two hills come close to the opposite shores of the Mohawk. Ancient people used antlers from deer to chip the chert to create the projectile points.

One reason that the Amsterdam find is especially interesting is that the artifacts from the Mohawk era were found along the river. Conventional wisdom has been that the Mohawks lived primarily in upland settings, not along the river.

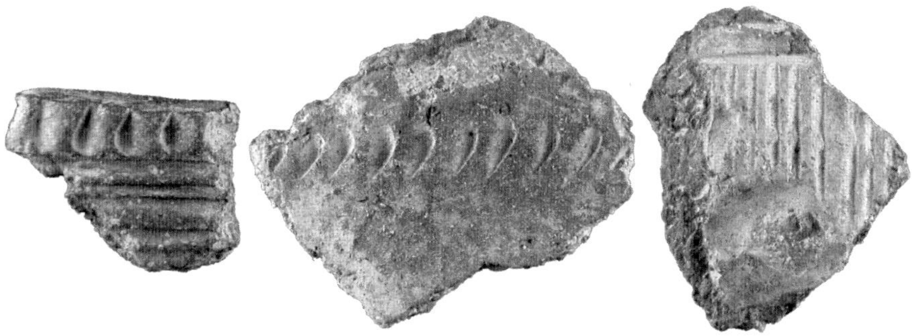

Five-hundred-year old Mohawk Nation ceramic sherds from the Amsterdam archaeological dig. *The Louis Berger Group.*

The next picture displays three fragments, or sherds, of ceramics from the Mohawk era about five hundred years ago, before the first contact with Europeans. Gould said Native Americans developed ceramics about three thousand years ago, learning how to make cooking utensils and other objects from clay, which became hardened when subjected to fire.

Gould and his team found the ancient objects and other items from the 1800s while doing preliminary work for a planned pedestrian bridge over the Mohawk River in Amsterdam, scheduled to be built with money the state would borrow as part of a Transportation Bond Act. Work at the Chuctanunda Terrace Site was expected to continue.

The artifacts were studied in 2011 at a Louis Berger Group facility in Iowa. The New York State Museum in Albany, in cooperation with the Mohawk Nation, will have ultimate responsibility for disposition of the artifacts. The director of the Walter Elwood Museum in Amsterdam, Ann Peconie, is hopeful some of the objects can be displayed there. Others have suggested that a display be created at the city's Riverlink Park in conjunction with the pedestrian bridge.

Chuctanunda

There are two creeks that flow almost opposite each other into the Mohawk River at Amsterdam: the North Chuctanunda and the South Chuctanunda.

One theory on the unusual name was that it meant "Twin Sisters," referring to the two creeks. Historians Gerald Snyder and Robert von Hasseln say it is more likely that the name means "stony place of shelter." Rocks overhang the spot where the North Chuctanunda empties into the river.

To confuse things a bit, locally the North Chuctanunda is frequently referred to simply as the Chuctanunda. The North Chuctanunda, also called the "Chuck" or the "Chuck-them-under," was key to industrial development, at first providing a source of power for local mills. The creek flows south from Galway Lake and runs for about seventeen miles to the river.

In the heyday of Amsterdam industry, the North Chuctanunda was terribly polluted by carpet dye and other chemicals. Especially in summer, the creek gave off a sickening odor. In winter, it looked something like Spumoni ice cream, according to one account, as different layers of colored dye would freeze in the cold weather. Since heavy industry abandoned the city, the creek has become cleaner. In recent years, periodic cleanup efforts and creek tours have been led by retired teacher John Naple of the Montgomery County Water Quality Coordinating Committee.

THE VALLEY OF THE KANYENKEHAKA

The late historian Paul Keesler came to the conclusion that our valley got its name in the Mohawk language from what are popularly known as Herkimer diamonds. Keesler's posthumously published book is *Mohawk—Discovering the Valley of the Crystals*. The title is based on research Keesler believes explains the origin of the word Kanyenkehaka, which is what the Mohawks called themselves. Kanyenka was their name for the Mohawk Valley.

The word *Mohawk* is a European corruption of a rival tribe's slur. "The Mohican Indians living in the upper Hudson Valley called their enemies, who lived in the valley to their west, Mohowaug—they eat living creatures," Keesler said. For years, the common wisdom was that *Kanyenkehaka* meant "People of the Flint," and *Kanyenka* meant the "Place of the Flint." Flint was important to Native Americans for making cutting-edge tools and weapons, but no major source of flint has been found in the area.

Keesler came to the conclusion that the Mohawks' name for themselves meant "People of the Crystals," and the name for their homeland meant "Place of the Crystals." The late University at Albany anthropologist Dean Snow pointed out that the valley is a major source of clear quartz crystals embedded in dolostone rocks. These crystals are called Herkimer diamonds

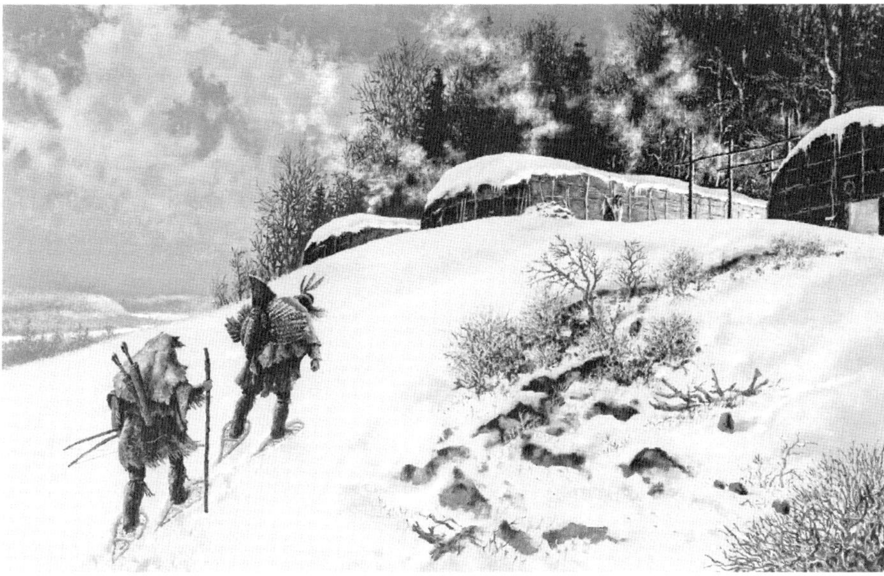

Winter in the Valley of the Mohawks, by Len Tantillo.

today, and there is a tourist site north of Herkimer where people look for these "diamonds."

"Crystals were symbolically important as amulets of success, health and long life," Keesler said. "The Mohawks were the main suppliers of quartz crystals up to 1644."

Keesler explored the 161 miles of the river from Rome to Waterford, 30 miles on foot and the rest by canoe, for his last book. Unlike some in the western Mohawk Valley, Keesler realized the importance of the eastern Mohawk Valley. Although other historians are skeptical, Keesler believed that Wolf Hollow, east of Cranesville, was the site of the last battle between the Mohawks and the Algonquins in 1669. The Algonquins had been driven off after attacking a Mohawk settlement near today's Fonda. The Mohawks pursued their enemy to Wolf Hollow and ambushed them.

If there is a dividing line between the eastern and western Mohawk Valley, it is probably at the Noses. Two large hills east of Canajoharie and west of Fonda frame the narrowest section of the valley floor. The Mohawk River/Erie Canal, railroad, New York State Thruway and Routes 5 and 5S all pass through the small gap between the Noses. Looking west, Little Nose is on the left and Big Nose is on the right. Keesler climbed both.

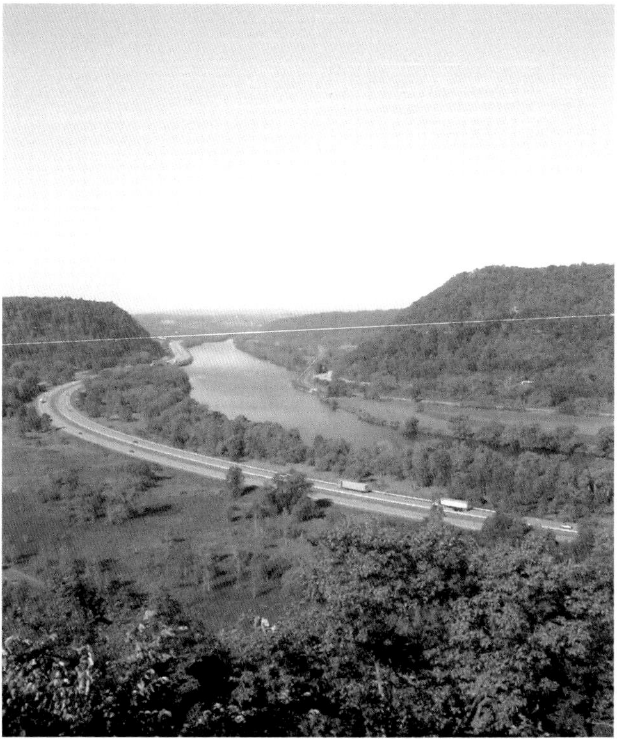

The narrowest gap in the Mohawk Valley is formed by Little Nose (left) and Big Nose (right). The view looks west toward Canajoharie. *Paul Keesler.*

"Despite the abundance of trees, we photographed the valley in both directions," Keesler wrote after climbing to the top of Big Nose. "Spectacular!"

Keesler also explored the river's tributaries in the eastern Mohawk Valley, including the Schoharie Creek, which enters the Mohawk at Fort Hunter. He researched the meaning of the word *Schoharie*, an Indian word that he found meant "Driftwood" or "Flood Wood." Driftwood used to collect on the Schoharie Creek where two smaller streams enter, forming a natural bridge during high water.

Keesler said, "Today there are few huge trees along the river to anchor such a log pile, and farmers who grow corn in these rich bottomlands would never tolerate a schoharie."

Originally an air traffic controller for the Federal Aviation Administration, Keesler began his writing career in 1966 with a magazine article about fishing on West Canada Creek. For several years, he wrote the outdoors column for the *Utica Observer Dispatch*. In 1972, he founded the *Mid York Sportsman* magazine, which became the *New York Sportsman* in 1975. In 1992, he retired as editor of the magazine.

In 1999, he wrote "Kuyahoora—Discovering West Canada Valley," describing the history and wildlife of the valley of the West Canada Creek, which flows into the Mohawk River at Herkimer. *Kuyahoora*, meaning "Leaping Waters," was the Indian name for the creek because of a spectacular waterfall. Keesler lived in Newport, along the creek. He died in 2005.

The Painted Rocks

The Painted Rocks were on the north shore of the Mohawk River in Amsterdam, near the former New York Central Railroad freight station and the mouth of the North Chuctanunda Creek. Speculation is that the rocks may have been painted by the Mohawks. By the late 1800s, the rock face drawings were no longer visible.

Canajoharie artist Rufus Grider painted several watercolors of the Painted Rocks in 1887, relying on testimony from people who remembered the originals. According to a newspaper article written by Grider, John Winnie of Amsterdam recalled that twelve or fifteen Indians and two canoes were depicted traveling west, with a duck flying above in the opposite direction. Another witness said that the rocks were painted red. A third reported that the human figures were about four feet high and could be seen from the other side of the river.

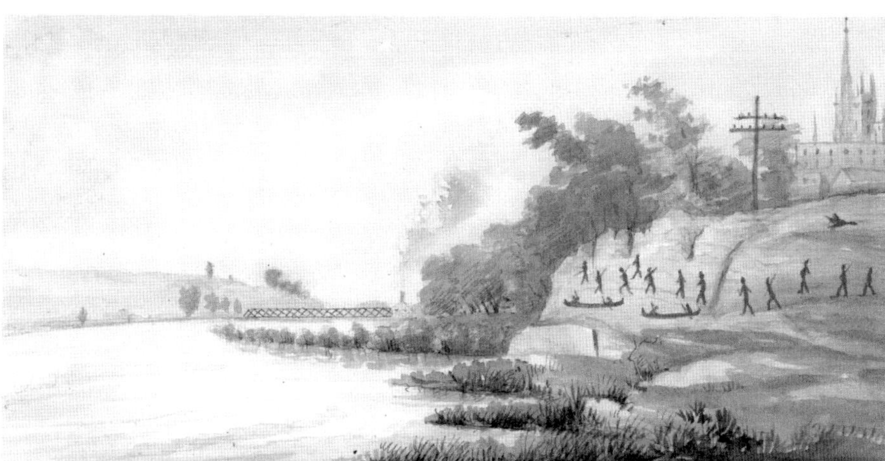

Rufus Grider's depiction of the Painted Rocks in Amsterdam, painted in 1887. *New York State Archives.*

Grider had moved to Canajoharie in 1883, when he was sixty-six, to teach art at Canajoharie Academy. A widower, Grider was raised in a Moravian community in Pennsylvania, had operated an inn and also taught art in Philadelphia, according to an authority on the artist, Alice Smith Duncan of Canajoharie.

Grider created more than two thousand Mohawk Valley drawings that are an important guide to local history. He also painted watercolors of powder horns used in colonial wars and the American Revolution. The powder horns were decorated with images and text, a practice similar to how airmen drew pictures on airplanes in World War II. Grider also copied eighteenth-century deeds, maps and other documents.

Active in history societies, he was instrumental in restoration of the 1740s-era Van Alstyne Homestead on Moyer Street in Canajoharie. Occupied by Philip Van Alstyne during the American Revolution, the homestead was a meeting place for the Tryon County Militia.

Grider had seen how the steel industry changed the landscape in Pennsylvania, according to Smith Duncan, and he began making representational paintings of Mohawk Valley scenes that had already disappeared or were likely to disappear.

Smith Duncan calls Grider's technique of interviewing old-timers, as he did in the case of the Painted Rocks, "forensic documentation." Sometimes his interview subjects signed the pictures, indicating the artist had accurately rendered their memories. Grider frequently wrote narratives to accompany the paintings.

"As you go through the valley, every small historical society has one or several Griders," Smith Duncan said. "He wasn't trained as an artist on a sophisticated level. His impulse was historical."

Grider wrote:

> *Having a taste for historical matters, and finding that the Valley was rich in such, I obtained the books giving the history thereof, and then began to visit the places of historic interest spoken of, frequently traversing the country on foot.*
>
> *One of the historians whose work I read,* [Jeptha] *Simms, regretted that so much had been lost because no limner had put the appearance of these historic places and buildings on record. While the historians were able to write and describe, they were not able to sketch. That opened up a field for me, as I was able to do such work.*

When Grider died in 1900, he left nine scrapbooks with pen and ink drawings and watercolors of Mohawk Valley scenes that are now housed at the State Library in Albany. Other Griders are at institutions in Canajoharie, Fonda, Fort Johnson, New York City and elsewhere. And, Smith Duncan said, the artist left an equally large body of work in Pennsylvania.

The day Grider died, he was scheduled to do a talk that night. He had done his last painting a little more than a month before. Reading his obituary, Smith Duncan said, you can tell he was a "known commodity" in Canajoharie—friendly, generous and well liked. One of his daughters married into the locally prominent Sammons family.

"He was the most prolific, productive person you can imagine," Smith Duncan said.

Sir William Johnson and Slavery

Sir William Johnson arguably was the most important European colonial figure in the Mohawk Valley. Johnson came to America in 1738 from Ireland. He constructed a fortified home in Fort Johnson and then a mansion in Johnstown, Johnson Hall.

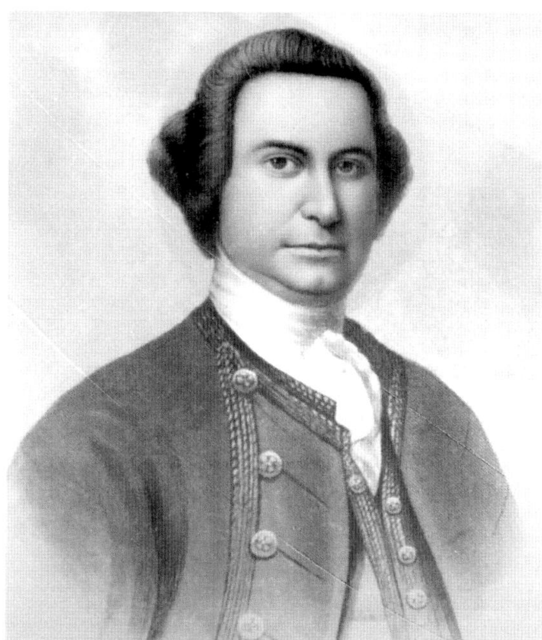

Sir William Johnson, a native of Ireland, British Indian agent in the Mohawk Valley and slave owner. *Montgomery County Dept. of History and Archives.*

As Britain's superintendent of Indian affairs, he was known for forging alliances by treating Native Americans fairly. He also owned at least forty slaves.

"We're talking about that period in history when the western frontier of the American colonies lay in the Mohawk River valley between Albany and what is now the city of Rome," said Wanda Burch, retired site manager at Johnson Hall in Johnstown.

Burch continued, "This was a region developed using the European plantation system, with large landowners and tenant farmers who produced agricultural goods in great quantities for the export market. For example, Mohawk Valley wheat was regularly shipped to the West Indies."

Johnson's slaves likely came from the British West Indies through agents in New York City. Burch said there is documentary evidence of at least forty slaves on Johnson's plantation, about ten household slaves and thirty field hands.

"This is a common misconception among the visitors who come into the Northeast," Burch said. "You say 'slavery' and they immediately think of the South. And they say, 'They had slaves here?' They definitely had slaves."

African American visitors seeking to study genealogy are frequently frustrated with the lack of information on the identities of the slaves.

Burch said:

> *For many years, I thought the Johnson family had simply given some of these slaves what seemed to me rather unusual names—things like Quacko and Jubah and, of course, Sambo, which we've heard in all sorts of controversy in later years. They seemed unusual. They were not. I later read some papers on the names of people coming from the British West Indies, and these were very common names. And then when I began speaking to other people who were working with eighteenth-century sites in the Northeast, these are very, very common names. So if someone comes looking to do genealogy, you might find a Cato in the Herkimer household; you might find the name in a New England household or at Johnson Hall. So that's not very helpful.*

Johnson's Mohawk wife, Molly Brant, took two of the family slaves with her as personal servants when she fled the Mohawk Valley for Canada during the American Revolution. By then, Johnson had died, but his family and his Mohawk friends supported the British side in the war.

The Mohawks and other Native Americans had mixed feelings about the fact that Johnson owned slaves. Burch said, "A couple of times we've got references to the slaves running away and seeking refuge among the Seneca and the Mohawk, who are nearby, and finding refuge there and then trying to stir up trouble. And at the same time, we find people such as Molly Brant holding slaves themselves."

Slavery began to die out after the Revolution in the Northeast. Loyalists, such as the Johnsons, owned some of the large plantation farms. These estates were broken up after the war ended, and slaves weren't as useful anymore.

"And you already had African American free men living in the northern colonies as opposed to the South," Burch said. "So it was a more gradual transition."

Imported Scots

In 1774, the year before he died, Sir William Johnson saw to it that hundreds of Scots came to his vast land estate, an area that today is occupied by the cities of Johnstown and Gloversville.

As a military leader, Johnson won a major battle against the French in 1755 at Lake George. After the victory, Johnson was made a baronet and granted 100,000 acres of land that the British had previously secured from the Mohawks. The land parcel was known as the Kingsborough Patent.

To populate this area, Johnson tapped into a tide of immigrants from the highlands of Scotland who were coming to America at a fast clip between 1770 and the American Revolution.

The Highlanders were a proud people who had strong loyalties to their clan chiefs. Many of their chiefs had been killed in the bloody but unsuccessful effort to install Prince Charles on the British throne in 1745.

The Highlanders' fierce but futile resistance had the unusual effect of convincing British authorities that Scottish soldiers would be effective in the British army as the empire expanded in America. Also, times were hard in Scotland, and many Highlanders simply opted to take a chance in the New World.

Johnson advertised leased land on his Kingsborough Patent through New York City agents and convinced four hundred Scots of the Highland Clan MacDonnell to settle on his property.

Many of these Scots arrived in 1773, some of them onboard a ship called the *Pearl*, which came to New York Harbor. The Highlanders arrived under four chiefs, and their land grants ranged from one hundred to five hundred acres each.

After Sir William died, many of his Scot tenants were drawn into the Revolutionary War on the British side. Some three hundred of them followed

Sir William's son John into exile in Canada when the war broke out and served in the King's Royal Regiment of New York, sometimes called Johnson's Greens or the Royal Yorkers. Their final stand was in 1781 near Johnstown itself.

Those who survived the war lost their lands in New York to the new government. The British granted the Highlanders lands in Ontario, Canada, where some of their descendants still reside.

Burch said people wonder why the Highlanders, who lost their own lands to the British, fought so fiercely for the British in the American Revolution. One explanation is that the Highlanders felt that in each case they were not fighting for or against someone—they were fighting for their homeland.

DID GEORGE WASHINGTON SIT HERE?

One of the oldest privies in the United States is on the grounds of Old Fort Johnson, the fortified dwelling built in what is now Fort Johnson, New York, by colonist Sir William Johnson in 1749.

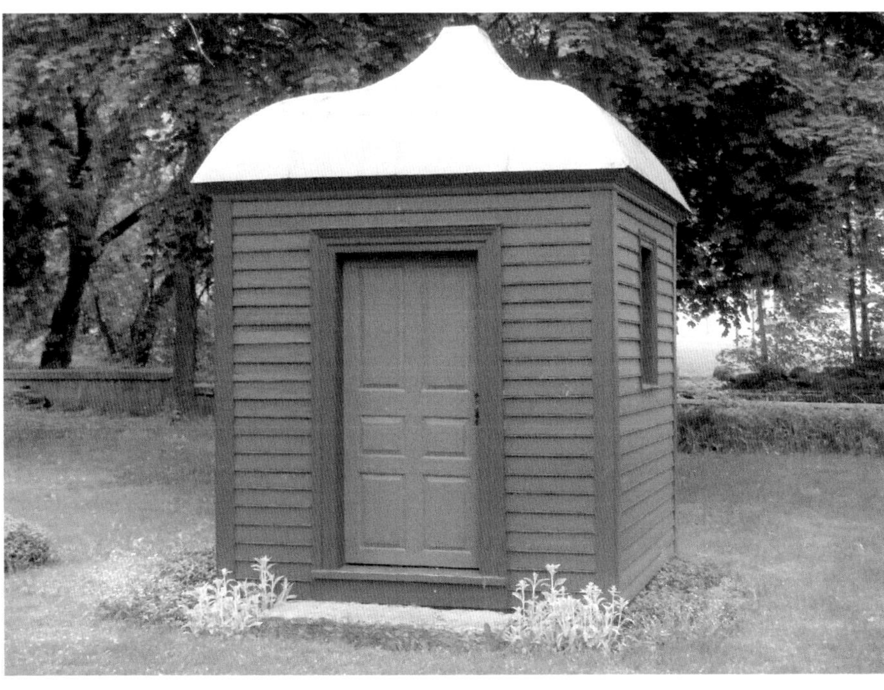

The restored privy at Old Fort Johnson. *Old Fort Johnson.*

"It is probably one of the top five outhouses in America," said Richard Strunk, of Windy Hill Restoration, whose firm restored the privy in recent years.

There are probably older privies preserved at Williamsburg, Virginia, and Winterthur, Delaware. But the Old Fort Johnson structure is one of a handful of existing outdoor toilets dating from the eighteenth century.

The Old Fort Johnson privy has two holes—not for simultaneous use as you might think, according to Strunk. Holes of different sizes were cut for different-sized bottoms. Strunk said small children were known to fall through or get stuck in outhouse holes meant for their elders.

The exact year of construction is not known. The privy is not shown on a detailed sketch of the buildings and grounds done by Guy Johnson, Sir William's nephew and son-in-law, in 1763. It is possible that Guy failed to sketch the privy because to do so would have been regarded as distasteful. Or the outhouse may have been built as part of the 1770 renovations undertaken by John Johnson, Sir William's son, to welcome his new high-society bride, Polly Watts of New York City.

"It is a very high-style structure," said Alessa Wylie, museum coordinator at the Old Fort Johnson Historic Landmark. The outhouse roof is vaulted, and the interior paneling matches paneling inside the Old Fort and other fine colonial homes.

Aaron Burr visited Old Fort Johnson soon after his marriage in 1782 with an eye on purchasing the building, which had been confiscated from the Loyalist Johnson family at the start of the Revolution. Burr never did buy the Old Fort but may have used the privy.

Did George Washington sit here? Washington visited the Fort Johnson area during his tour through the Mohawk Valley at the end of the Revolutionary War. Some believe that he might have visited the Old Fort and its privy at some point during his stopover.

Anxiety and boredom motivated George Washington to travel through the Mohawk Valley in 1783. Exactly where Washington visited is still a subject of dispute and conjecture.

Washington wrote to the Continental Congress from his headquarters in Newburgh in the Hudson Valley, saying that he was "teased with troublesome applications and fruitless demands." The war was over, but the peace treaty was months away. Washington told Congress that he would "wear away a little time in performing a tour of the Northward." After the trip, he made recommendations to improve local roads and fortifications.

A book about this trip—*General George Washington in the Mohawk Valley: Summer 1783*—was published in 2002 by two teachers, Deborah Skivington and her daughter, Beth Skivington.

According to the Skivingtons, Washington's account book for his trip documented a visit to a tavern in Fort Johnson. But the entry does not specifically state that he visited the Old Fort.

A century later, the privy entered the historical record once again. A sketch by artist E.L. Henry in the early 1880s showed the privy on a stone foundation built over a nearby creek. The sketch noted that the outhouse was a "dark brownish green" with a "red gray door."

The privy was moved to its current location away from the creek in the early twentieth century, after the building was acquired by the Montgomery County Historical Society, which today operates Old Fort Johnson as a museum.

ALBERT VEDDER AND JOSEPH HAGAMAN

What we know as the city of Amsterdam was a late arrival in the Mohawk Valley. And the exact year the settlement on the North Chuctanunda Creek got the name Amsterdam is in doubt.

When William Johnson constructed Fort Johnson in 1749, he built on the west shore of the creek near the fort with good reason. The land to the east, including the present city of Amsterdam, was part of a "fraudulently acquired" land patent or grant, according to Old Fort Johnson site manager Scott Haefner. The Kayaderosseras Patent supposedly contained 700,000 acres and was acquired from the provincial government by "some gentlemen of Albany" in 1708.

"The [land patent] system invited speculation by those with governmental influence, and colonial officialdom cut itself in on many shady deals," said historian Hugh Donlon. The Mohawk Indians thought they had ceded only enough land for a small farm in the Kayaderosseras Patent and refused to allow European settlement in the disputed area for sixty years. During that time, Haefner said, "The hamlets of Cranesville, Fort Johnson, Fort Hunter and Minaville were being settled."

William Johnson finally negotiated a deal with the Mohawks in 1768 that cut down the size of the disputed land grant and provided five thousand pounds for the tribe. Within a few years, the political landscape changed drastically as the Mohawks and Johnson's descendants fled the valley during the Revolutionary War. In 1793, four townships were created in the area: Johnstown, Broadalbin, Mayfield and Amsterdam.

The first settlements inside what is now the city of Amsterdam were made by Joseph Hagaman and Albert Vedder about 1783. Hagaman arrived first and marked his claim by leaving a load of stone next to the North Chuctanunda Creek, returning to Dutchess County for his family. When Hagaman came back, Haefner said, Vedder was occupying the location. Hagaman went four miles up the creek to found Hagaman's Mills, today the village of Hagaman.

Vedder had served during the Revolution in the third regiment of the Tryon County militia and was the first tenant shown living in Old Fort Johnson after the war, about the time he was building a sawmill and gristmill on the North Chuctanunda. The settlement that grew there was first called Vedder's Mills, and in 1794, it was renamed Veddersburg. Some people started calling the hamlet Amsterdam, the same name as the surrounding township and, of course, the capital of the Netherlands, where many residents traced their roots.

Sometime between 1804 and 1810, the hamlet's name was changed from Veddersburg to Amsterdam at a town meeting. Local lore has it that the meeting took place at town supervisor James Allen's inn on what is now Route 30, land that was to become Stephen Sanford's horse farm. Supposedly, Allen cast the deciding vote when the original ballot ended in a tie.

Historians differ on whether this meeting took place in 1804 or 1808. To add to the confusion, Amsterdam celebrated its centennial in 1910, but more recent observances, including the sesquicentennial of 1954 and the bicentennial of 2004, used 1804 as the name change year.

Haefner cited documentary evidence to back the 1808 date. The 1808 Amsterdam town meeting was to be held in the church at Veddersburg. In 1809, however, the town meeting was scheduled for the village of Amsterdam.

According to Haefner, Vedder was still alive in 1833, receiving a military pension from New York State at the age of seventy-three. Amsterdam officially incorporated as a village in 1830 and became a city in 1885.

Vedder's First Name

The late Amsterdam city historian James Marks found that some history books give Vedder's first name as Albert, but other sources use Aaron.

Marks said that in Germanic countries, the middle name was often used as the common name for a son if his father had the same first name. It would be the same idea as our practice of calling a son Junior to avoid confusion with his father, assuming his father has the same name.

Marks wrote, "In the Vedder family of Schenectady the name Albertse is often seen and indicates by the 'se' an ancestor named Albert. Arent, Arient [Aaron] are also very common. My guess would be that [the founder of Veddersburg] was Aaron Albertse Vedder and was called by whichever name confused people the least."

The Way West

Port Jackson on the Erie Canal

The Mohawk Valley is the best route by land and water through America's eastern mountains. According to the late historian Katherine Strobeck, Amsterdam became an important stop on the way west:

> *At the time that the West was being settled how could you get there except through the Mohawk Valley? You couldn't go through Pennsylvania because of the mountains. You couldn't go through the Carolinas because of the mountains. There were mountains all the way to Georgia. And that's why the Erie Canal was built.*

In the 1800s, what is now Amsterdam's South Side was originally named Stillwellville after John Stillwell, who operated two stores on the new canal. In 1835, the name of the settlement was changed to Port Jackson in honor of Samuel Jackson, a prosperous farmer and merchant. Port Jackson became a bustling, rowdy stop on the canal.

"The canal was terribly crowded," Strobeck said. "It was one boat right after another. Usually there was a fight at the lock to see who got through first."

Port Jackson had a canal basin, making it possible for boats to turn around and providing a place for boats to dock for unloading. The building that housed Sweet's Canal Store still exists and is on the National Register of

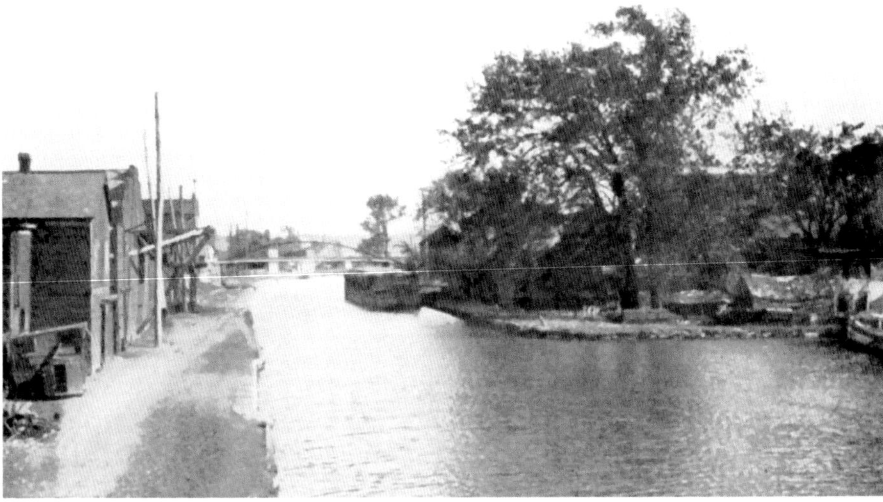

The Erie Canal in Amsterdam. Before 1888, the area the canal passed through was called Port Jackson. *Gerald B. Snyder.*

Historic Places. The original Erie Canal had to pass by aqueduct over creeks, and one such aqueduct was built to cross the South Chuctanunda Creek in Port Jackson.

The Erie Canal's commercial importance dwindled with the rise of the New York Central Railroad, which went through Amsterdam on the north side of the river. In 1888, the booming city of Amsterdam annexed Port Jackson.

The Schoharie Crossing State Historic Site in Fort Hunter shows the three stages of the Erie Canal—the original canal, an enlargement done in the 1830s and the current Erie/Barge Canal using the bed of the Mohawk River, where construction started in 1912. In 1915, the old Erie Canal ceased operations. The following year, the old canal was emptied. By 1918, the new Barge Canal was in operation, using the riverbed.

Sheldon Jackson and Alaska

The son of Port Jackson founder Samuel Jackson is credited with introducing reindeer to Alaska. According to research done by late Amsterdam city historian James Marks, Sheldon Jackson was born in 1834 in Minaville, a hamlet in the town of Florida, south of Amsterdam on today's State Route 30. Jackson is buried there in the Chuctanunda Cemetery.

Sheldon Jackson attended Union College and Princeton Theological Seminary, where he was graduated, ordained and married within one week in 1858.

Jackson wanted to be a foreign missionary but was turned down because of his short stature—he was just over five feet tall. Instead, he became a missionary on the American frontier. He established over one hundred churches and missions, including the first Presbyterian churches in Wyoming, Montana, Utah and Arizona.

In 1877, Jackson went to Alaska and, although he never permanently lived there, was appointed superintendent of education in the territory in 1885.

Jackson found that the natives were starving, writing:

> *The whales and walruses along the coast, which had for ages previous furnished their forefathers with an abundance of food supply, had been nearly destroyed by the American whale men. In the interior of the country, the introduction of loaded firearms was destroying the fur-bearing animals, which were used as food, more rapidly than they could increase.*

He visited Russia's Siberia, where he found that the natives relied on reindeer for food. Jackson raised funds to introduce reindeer as a source of food and clothing in Alaska. Sent by the U.S. government to Lapland and Norway in 1898, he purchased over five hundred reindeer and secured a colony of Laplanders to look after the animals until the Eskimos were trained in how to raise them.

In later years, Jackson lived in Washington, D.C., where he served with the Alaskan division of the U.S. Bureau of Education. He died in 1909. His name is remembered at churches and schools throughout the American West and Alaska.

Naming Minaville

The hamlet of Minaville, where Sheldon Jackson was born, is named for Spanish general Francis Mina, according to historian W. Max Reid in his Mohawk Valley history, written over one hundred years ago. Reid said that area businessman George Smith got Minaville adopted as the hamlet's name in 1818.

Mina was a Spanish guerilla who harassed the French under Napoleon in Spain and ultimately found his way to England, where he became interested in the cause of Mexican independence. Mina came to America and raised an army that stormed Mexico City. He won many battles but was ultimately captured and executed in Mexico in 1817.

Reid wrote, "This was the man for whom Minaville was named, not because he was a Spaniard, but because he was a brave man and the leader of American volunteers fighting for the independence of an alien nation."

Amsterdam's Benedict Arnold

Amsterdam's Benedict Arnold, buried at the city's Green Hill Cemetery, was not the Revolutionary War figure of the same name, a fact noted by the Library of Congress when the Mohawk Valley man died in 1849.

Could it be that Arnold, born on October 5, 1780, was named in honor of the famous general who became an infamous traitor? What seems more likely, according to local historian Alessa Wylie, is that Benedict was simply an often-used name in the good Benedict Arnold's family.

Patriot general Benedict Arnold and Richard Montgomery tried but failed to conquer Quebec City at the end of 1775. Montgomery died in that battle, and Montgomery County, where Amsterdam is located, is named in Montgomery's honor, as are counties in sixteen other states. There is a monument to General Arnold's leg at the Saratoga battleground, as he was badly wounded in the leg in that 1777 battle. General Arnold was regarded as a hero until his plans to betray the fort at West Point were found out on September 23, 1780.

The man who became Amsterdam's Benedict Arnold was born less than two weeks later, on October 5 of that year. One source reports that our Benedict Arnold was born in Rennselaer County, while others list his birthplace as Florida, just south of Amsterdam, or Amsterdam itself.

By 1808, Arnold was operating a general store at Bridge and Main Streets in Amsterdam. He was in the Ninth Cavalry of the New York State Militia during the War of 1812, described in local accounts as a major general. He was Amsterdam town supervisor from 1813 to 1816 and then a state assemblyman in 1817 and 1818. Arnold was one of the founders of the Amsterdam Aqueduct Company in 1829. The company laid pipes west of the Chuctanunda Creek to bring water to thirsty citizens.

Arnold was a member of Congress from 1829 to 1831, during the administration of President Andrew Jackson, although he was politically opposed to Jackson.

When Arnold returned from Washington, he was among those who led the campaign to incorporate Amsterdam as a village. He was the second president of the village board in 1832. He was Town of Amsterdam supervisor again from 1835 to 1836 and, in 1844, was one of the organizers of the Fonda Fair. At some point, he owned a distillery whose vats were purchased the year he died for what became Kelloggs and Miller, a local linseed oil manufacturer.

Arnold's Market Street home was a landmark torn down for the construction of the Blood Building, now the site of the Best Western Hotel.

Arnold died on March 3, 1849, and was buried in a cemetery on Market Hill. Later, his remains were moved to Green Hill Cemetery.

Also buried at Green Hill is Arnold's grandson, Lieutenant Benedict Arnold Leonard, who was killed in 1864 in the Battle of Spotsylvania Court House, the lieutenant's twelfth Civil War battle. He was an officer in the Thirty-second and Seventy-third New York Volunteer Infantry.

Arnold Avenue and the former Arnold Avenue School, built in 1891, were named in honor of the good Benedict Arnold and his family.

Green Hill

The Arnold graves are two among many important historic markers at Green Hill Cemetery, opened in 1858 and expanded in 1865. Green Hill was designed by Burton A. Thomas, who also designed Vale Cemetery in Schenectady and Albany Rural Cemetery. These and other so-called rural cemeteries were not only places to bury the dead but also public parks.

Other famous Amsterdamians buried at Green Hill include carpet maker Stephen Sanford and members of his family. Many of the families whose businesses helped create Amsterdam's industrial prosperity are memorialized at Green Hill, names such as Kellogg, Morris, Sugden, Voorhees, Wallins and McLeary.

The cemetery, listed on the State and National Registers of Historic Places, is at Church and Cornell Streets in Amsterdam, adjacent to city hall.

Amsterdam and Its Railroads

In 1836, the first train of the Schenectady & Utica Railroad arrived in Amsterdam. For three decades after that, there was no Amsterdam train station. Passengers waited for trains at the Railroad Hotel at the end of Railroad Street, just west of where Route 30 crosses East Main Street in Amsterdam today.

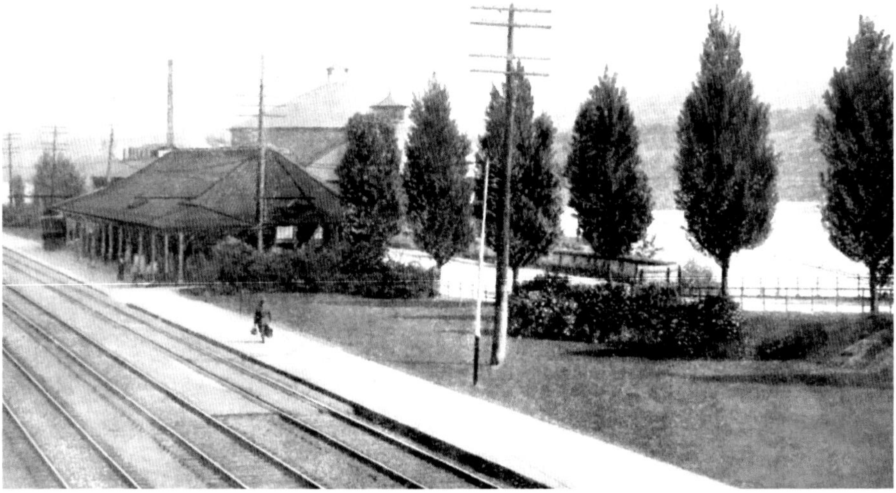

The Amsterdam train station occupied land between the railroad tracks and the river from 1899 until demolition in the late 1960s. *Gerald B. Snyder.*

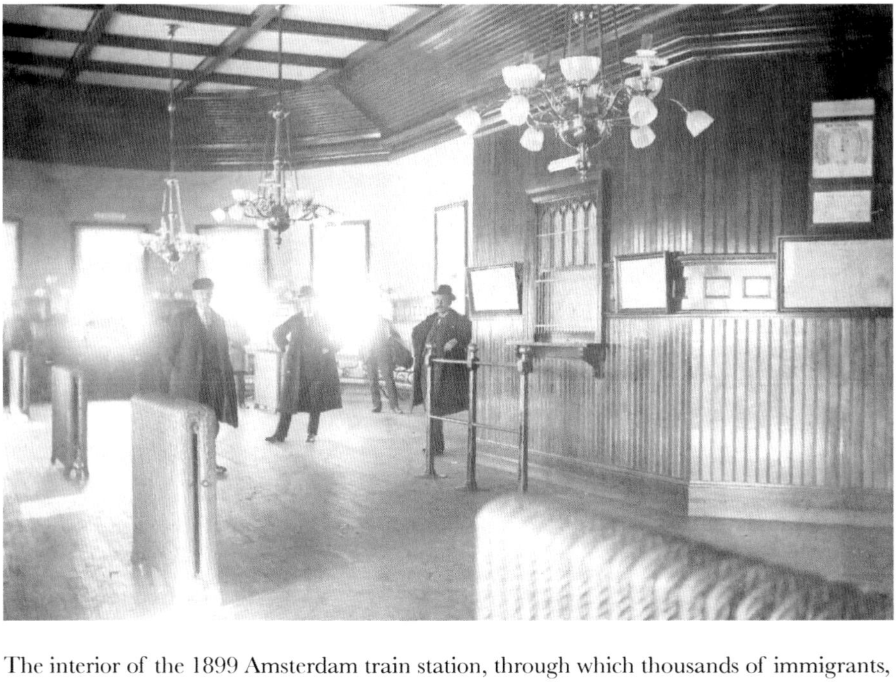

The interior of the 1899 Amsterdam train station, through which thousands of immigrants, salespeople and other travelers passed. *Gerald B. Snyder.*

A train station for passengers and freight was built there on the north side of the tracks in 1867, two years before the New York Central & Hudson River Railroad was formed. Carpet maker Stephen Sanford contributed an ornate fountain that beautified the site for some thirty years. The fountain was later moved to St. Mary's Church on East Main Street but was removed from there in the 1940s.

In 1899, a more substantial passenger train depot was built on the south side of the railroad tracks for $60,000. Vehicle access was provided by a ramp built between an overhead railroad crossing and the Mohawk River bridge that connected the north and south sides of the city. That station was demolished in 1970 as part of urban renewal, and the current Amtrak station was built in the West End of Amsterdam.

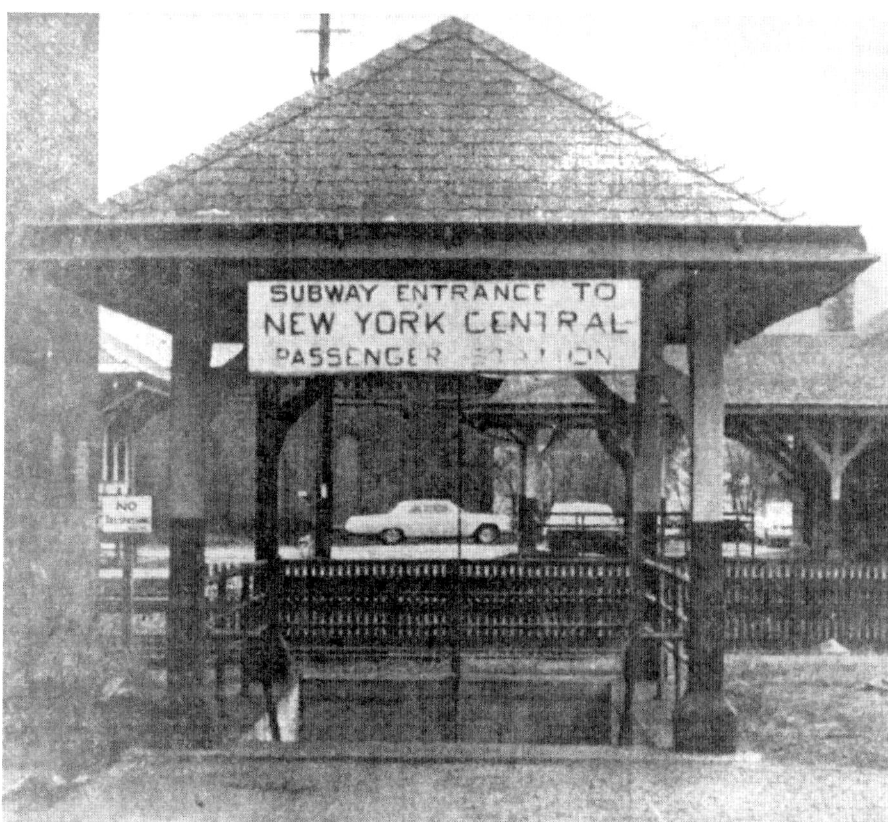

The urine-soaked subway entrance to the Amsterdam passenger train station was demolished along with the station building in 1970. Recorder *newspaper.*

During the peak of rail travel, twenty-seven trains a day stopped in Amsterdam. Soldiers left for two world wars from the station. Joe DiMaggio and the New York Yankees arrived there in 1942 to play their farm team, the Amsterdam Rugmakers.

Pedestrians could reach the train station through a tunnel under the tracks at the foot of Railroad Street. That leaky and foul-smelling tunnel became an icon itself in the 1950s. I remember rushing through the underground passageway with my mother on nights when sister Arlene was arriving for home visits from college in Potsdam. The tunnel was like an Amsterdam version of the catacombs.

West Shore

Starting in 1883, there was competition to the New York Central from the New York, West Shore & Buffalo Railroad. The West Shore was so named for the side of the Hudson River on which it operated. In the Mohawk Valley, the West Shore tracks were on the south side of the Mohawk River.

The West Shore had its own passenger depot on Amsterdam's South Side, near Bridge Street, although its passenger traffic was never as brisk as that of the New York Central. The West Shore did transport thousands of pilgrims to the Auriesville Shrine west of Amsterdam in the summer months. The West Shore's Amsterdam passenger depot was torn down in 1936.

Rail Freight

A few years after the New York Central built its Amsterdam passenger station in 1898, the railroad spent $1 million to expand the freight house at the foot of Hamilton Street, according to historian Hugh Donlon. Railway Express freight service was offered just east of the passenger station.

Amsterdam also boasts its own railroad short line: the Amsterdam, Chuctanunda & Northern, begun in 1879. This rail spur about a mile east of the city limits is still in operation today, according to the Amsterdam Industrial Development Agency. A good part of the line has been abandoned, but the remaining section is used to take freight to the Edson Street Industrial Park.

Historian Donlon said that the little railroad did a lot to save wear and tear on Amsterdam's streets. At its peak, the rail line could take freight cars to the former Mohawk Carpet upper mill complex, Bigelow Sanford's carpet mill, the Kelloggs & Miller linseed oil plant on Church Street, the Wytrwal Coal Company and John J. Turner Construction.

THE FONDA, JOHNSTOWN & GLOVERSVILLE RAILROAD

The history of the Fonda, Johnstown & Gloversville (FJ&G) Railroad is intertwined with the history of our region. There were two parts to the FJ&G: a steam and ultimately diesel railroad augmented by trucks and an electric division that ended as a bus line.

The steam railroad ran from the New York Central railhead in Fonda to Johnstown and Gloversville, with branches to Northville and Broadalbin. The steam line operated an amusement park—Sacandaga Park—that was flooded in 1930, when the Sacandaga Reservoir was created. The last train on the FJ&G ran in 1984.

The electric trolley era in American transportation was relatively brief. However, before the automobile became popular, trolley lines made it possible for workers to live in housing developments miles away from the factories where they worked.

The first electric car to operate in Fulton County ran in 1893 between Gloversville and Johnstown. Initially, the Cayadutta Electric Railroad provided trolley service. In 1894, the FJ&G leased the Cayadutta and the FJ&G, Cayadutta and Amsterdam Street Railroad consolidated as the FJ&G Railroad Company in 1902.

The electric line provided local trolley service in Gloversville, Johnstown and Amsterdam plus connected these cities and Fonda with interurban

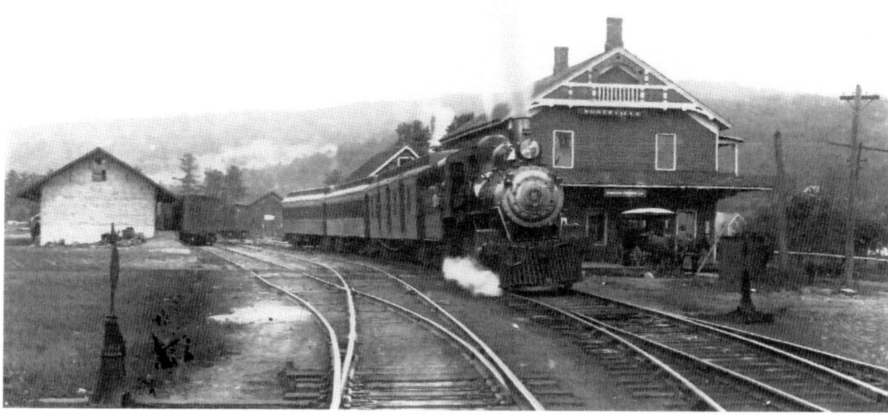

FJ&G passenger train #8 leaving Northville in a 1920 postcard image. *Paul K. Larner.*

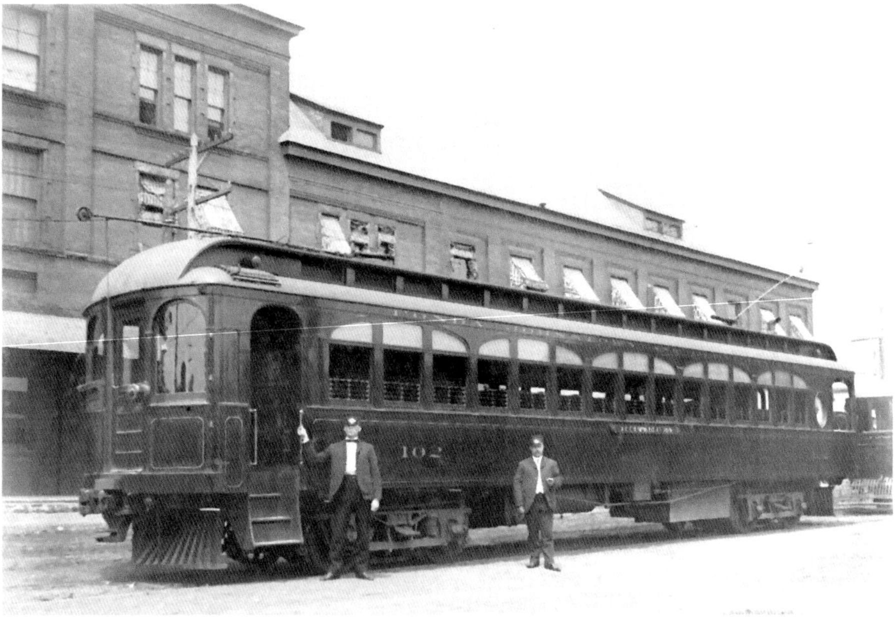

An interurban FJ&G electric car at Gloversville passenger station, about 1904. Motorman Asa Brower is near the front. *Company photo from Paul K. Larner.*

service. From its peak in 1903 to 1938, the FJ&G ran electric cars from Gloversville to Schenectady. The company provided bus service until 1956.

Gloversville native Paul K. Larner, a retired Amtrak locomotive engineer who lives in St. Albans Bay, Vermont, has published volume one of a history of the FJ&G called *Our Railroad (1867 to 1893)*.

"That's how Gloversville and Johnstown backers referred to the railroad at the beginning," Larner said.

In late 1892, New York Central interests obtained control of the railroad, selling out at a large profit to a group with interests in electric generation and developers of the Cayadutta Electric Railroad in June 1893. These men operated the company until it failed in 1932 under excessive debt incurred by extending the electric division to Schenectady. Emerging from reorganization in 1944, the FJ&G once again became "our railroad," under local ownership.

The FJ&G story involves political intrigue, regional differences and boardroom machinations. The railroad's history parallels the rise and fall of the region's major industries, especially in Fulton County.

"My goal is a thorough history," Larner said. His book uses detailed newspaper accounts that describe, for example, how prominent nineteenth-century Fulton County citizens such as Willard Heacock and Nicholas Decker vied for control of the companies that made up the FJ&G.

Republican Heacock, a judge and assemblyman from Gloversville, was instrumental in the creative financing that made the FJ&G steam railroad a reality in 1870. Decker, a political opponent of Heacock, started a horse railroad in 1874 to compete with the FJ&G. A traffic war between the competing forms of transportation took place. Ultimately, the FJ&G leased the horse railroad.

Larner has been a rail fan since his youth and began his railroad career with the FJ&G in 1964. In terms of FJ&G history, Larner said, "I owe everything to Dave." The late David F. Nestle wrote a history book in 1958 called *Steam and Trolley Days on the FJ&G*." Nestle, a high school teacher in Greenwich from 1959 through 1987, was well known as a railroad historian. His widow, Pat Nestle, donated her husband's extensive FJ&G picture collection to Fulton Montgomery Community College.

THE MILLS

THE SANFORDS OF AMSTERDAM

The Sanford family was instrumental in making Amsterdam the "Carpet City." However, the abrupt departure of Bigelow-Sanford in 1955 was the starting point of an era of economic decline.

The first member of the family to move to Amsterdam was John Sanford, born in Roxbury, Connecticut, in 1803. As a young man, he migrated to Amsterdam, where he became a teacher and merchant. He served a term in Congress from 1841 to 1843.

After John Sanford came home from Washington, he went into the carpet-manufacturing business. He brought his son Stephen into the firm the next year, making Stephen leave West Point, where he was studying for a military career. Stephen, born in 1826, took control of the business in 1855; his father died in 1857.

Stephen Sanford made the family carpet business prosper but did not ignore public service. He had become a friend of Ulysses S. Grant at West Point. A Republican, Sanford served one term in Congress from 1869 to 1871, during Grant's first presidential term.

According to historian Hugh Donlon, Sanford did not enjoy Congress, saying, "It is a thankless job to work for the public and I have had enough of it." Late in life, though, Sanford told a gathering of Amsterdam businessmen, "I look back with very great pleasure and satisfaction to the time I was in politics."

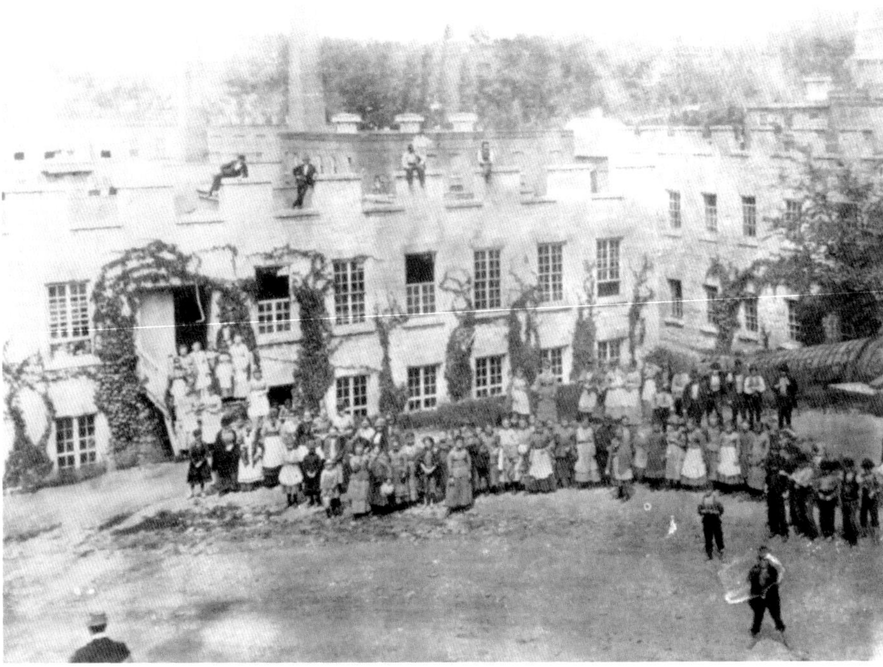

Workers pose around Sanford & Sons carpet mill at Amsterdam's Church and Prospect Streets in the 1800s. *Bob Cudmore.*

Sanford married Sarah Jane Cochrane of New York City in 1849. Their son John, born in 1851, served two terms in Congress as a Republican from 1889 to 1893 while Benjamin Harrison was president.

Stephen Sanford & Sons was at the head of Amsterdam's growing list of captains of industry in the late 1800s. There was competition, of course, from mills that made a variety of other products: knit goods, brooms, buttons, etc. And there was competition in the floor-covering business. The Shuttleworth brothers had come to Amsterdam from England in the late 1870s to weave carpets at a mill in the East End, near the Mohawk River. Former Sanford employees William McCleary, Samuel Wallin and David Crouse founded their own carpet mill—the Upper Mill—in the 1880s.

Fast Horses

In the 1870s, Stephen Sanford's doctor advised the industrialist that he was working too hard and encouraged him to take up farming as a hobby to help with what may have been stomach ulcers. Sanford started buying over one thousand acres of property that would become Hurricana Farm off what is now Route 30 in the town of Amsterdam. The name Hurricana derives from the strong winds that blow through the hilltop location.

Originally, Stephen Sanford bred draft horses at the farm. But his sons—John and William—encouraged their father to raise thoroughbreds because of their own interest in fast horses, especially jumpers. William died in 1896.

Sanford horses became fixtures at the nearby Saratoga racetrack. Trainer Hollie Hughes would lead a contingent to walk the horses from Hurricana to the Saratoga track each summer. An Amsterdam native and longtime associate of the Sanfords, Hughes was inducted into the National Racing Hall of Fame in 1973, and a race is named in his honor at Aqueduct.

In 1901, Sarah Jane Sanford died. Also that year, Sanford built his own stable on Nelson Avenue in Saratoga. He had as many as thirty-five horses at a time. When asked why he kept so many horses, the industrialist replied that he was not in the horse-raising business for "margin"—in other words, for profit.

From 1903 through 1907, the Sanfords invited the people of Amsterdam to the Sanford Matinee Races at Hurricana on the Sunday closest to the Fourth of July. There was food, drink, music and, of course, horse racing. Some fifteen thousand people attended the event during its last year.

"I read in the papers about General Sanford, the sporting man," Sanford said in 1906. "I never presumed to be a sporting man, but I am proud of it. Call me a sporting man if you like."

New York State outlawed betting in 1907, and racing stopped at Saratoga. Temporarily, the Sanfords sold most of their horses, according to historian Alex Robb in his book *The Sanfords of Amsterdam*.

Stephen Sanford was at least partially blind during the last five years of his life. The old gentleman doted on his grandchildren, in particular his namesake, born in 1899. He gave the boy a Shetland pony almost before the youngster could walk. Young Stephen called the pony Laddie. The grandfather bestowed the nickname "Laddie" on his grandson.

Stephen Sanford died on February 13, 1913. Six months later, racing resumed at Saratoga, along with the first running of the Sanford Memorial, still a fixture at Saratoga today.

According to Robb, John Sanford inherited $40 million at his father's death. He continued to head the carpet mill and operate the racing stable.

The farm produced many famous thoroughbreds, including 1916 Kentucky Derby winner George Smith—trained by Hollie Hughes. In the

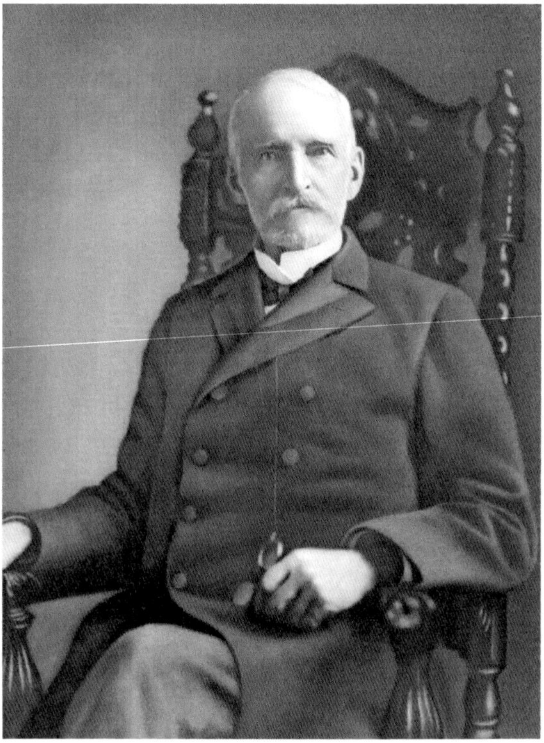

Amsterdam carpet manufacturer Stephen Sanford. When he died in 1913, he left $40 million to his son. *Old Fort Johnson.*

1920s, the farm's name was changed to Sanford Stud Farm. Twelve stone markers on the highway in front of the farm memorialized the names and victories of Sanford horses: Chuctanunda, Molly Brandt, Caughnawaga, Rockton, etc. Today, the monuments are disassembled and behind one of the remaining buildings.

In 1929, Sanford & Sons merged with Bigelow-Hartford, a New England carpet manufacturer, to form Bigelow-Sanford. John Sanford and his family were spending more and more time in Florida and other locations outside Amsterdam. In 1932, Sanford gave the family's Church Street mansion to the City of Amsterdam. It has been the city hall ever since.

On January 9, 1939, a fire killed twenty-five thoroughbred horses and did $200,000 damage at the Sanford Stud Farm. Newspaper accounts indicated that a fifteen-year old exercise boy, William H. Dougrey from Glens Falls, started the fire by disposing of his lighted cigarette inside the barn.

John Sanford died eight months after the horse barn fire. John's son, Stephen "Laddie" Sanford, who had become a famous horseman, and two of John's daughters took over the farm.

Lou Hildebrandt

Amsterdam native Louis Hildebrandt cut carrots for the horses and performed other menial tasks on his way to becoming a jockey for the Sanfords in the 1940s. Hildebrandt said that Sanford Stud Farm was its own little village, as so many exercise boys, grooms and other workers came from out of town.

In World War II, Hildebrandt served at a U.S. Army horse-training unit in Fort Robinson, Nebraska, with then army captain Laddie Sanford. After the war, Hildebrandt won important races for the Sanfords, including the Monmouth Park Handicap in New Jersey aboard Sanford's big horse, Roundview, in July 1947. Hildebrandt had been injured several times and reluctantly left the sport later that year. The horse farm manager starting in 1950 was Ray Pischel.

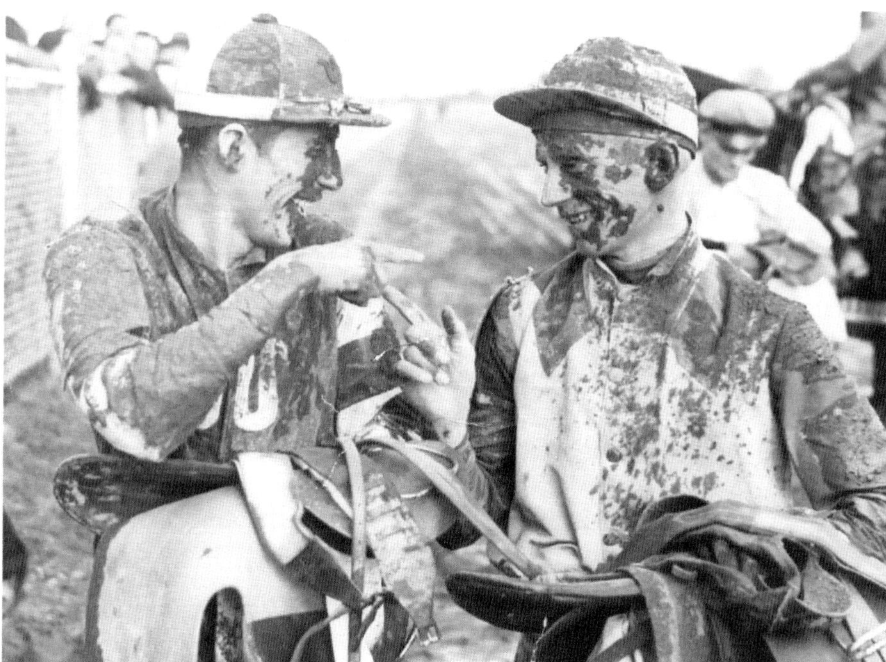

Jockeys Manny Garza and Lou Hildebrandt (right) in the 1940s. An Amsterdam native, Hildebrandt was a jockey for the Sanford Stud Farm. *Sam Hildebrandt.*

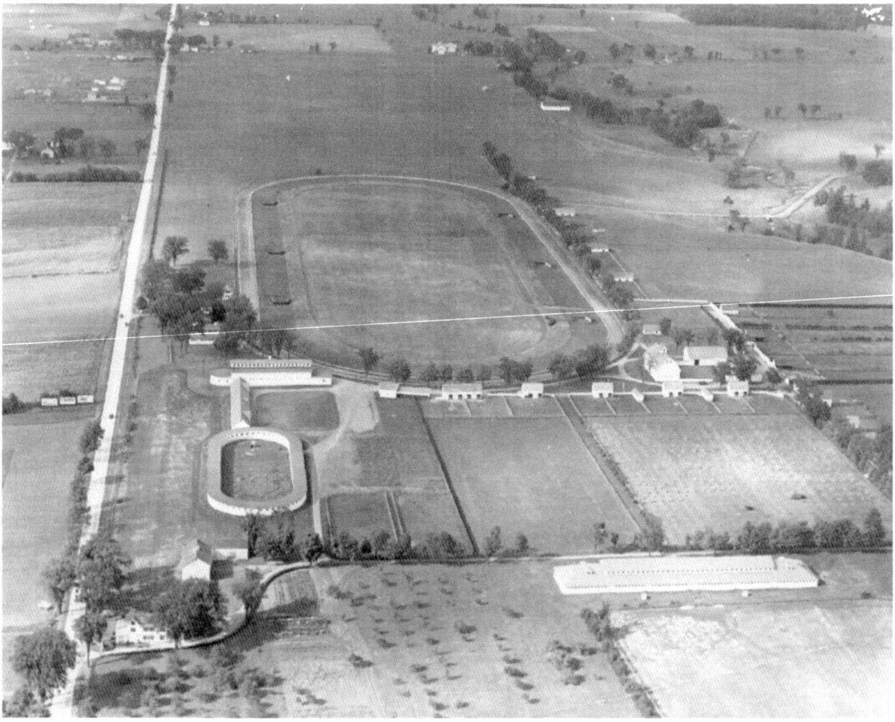

An aerial view of the Sanford Stud Farm in the town of Amsterdam, about 1940. *Sam Hildebrandt.*

1955

The January 1955 announcement that Bigelow-Sanford Carpet Company was leaving Amsterdam for Thompsonville, Connecticut, shocked Amsterdam residents and brought temporary joy to the residents of Thompsonville. The move eliminated 1,650 jobs in Amsterdam, most of them employed in making Axminster carpet.

New York governor Averill Harriman publicly pressured Laddie Sanford, then the company's largest stockholder, to do what he could to save jobs in Sanford's native Amsterdam. But Sanford, then living in Florida, told reporters, "Conditions in the carpet industry are very bad, making it necessary for us to cut down on our overhead."

In October 1955, more than two million square feet of Bigelow-Sanford's factory space was divided into twenty-one parcels and offered for sale at an Amsterdam auction, along with company houses and vacant lots. Property assessed at $5 million brought total bids of only $300,000.

The Sanford Stud Farm was put up for sale in 1976, the year before Laddie Sanford died. Most of the acreage has been used for development of big box and other retail stores. A group called the Friends of the Sanford Stud Farm has been working to restore what remains of the farm buildings, especially the Broodmare Barn and Jumping Horse Barn.

The Looms of Mohawk

There is a determined but jaunty tone to a 1943 newsletter called the *Mohawker*, published by Mohawk Mills for its employees and over nine hundred men and women from the factory who were scattered all over the world in the armed forces.

"Silent Mike Domkowski has his over-age discharge," began one of the items describing workers from Mohawk's Wilton Department. "His Sergeant told him he'd do more good for the Army in civilian life than being in it. Mike said: 'I ain't mad.'"

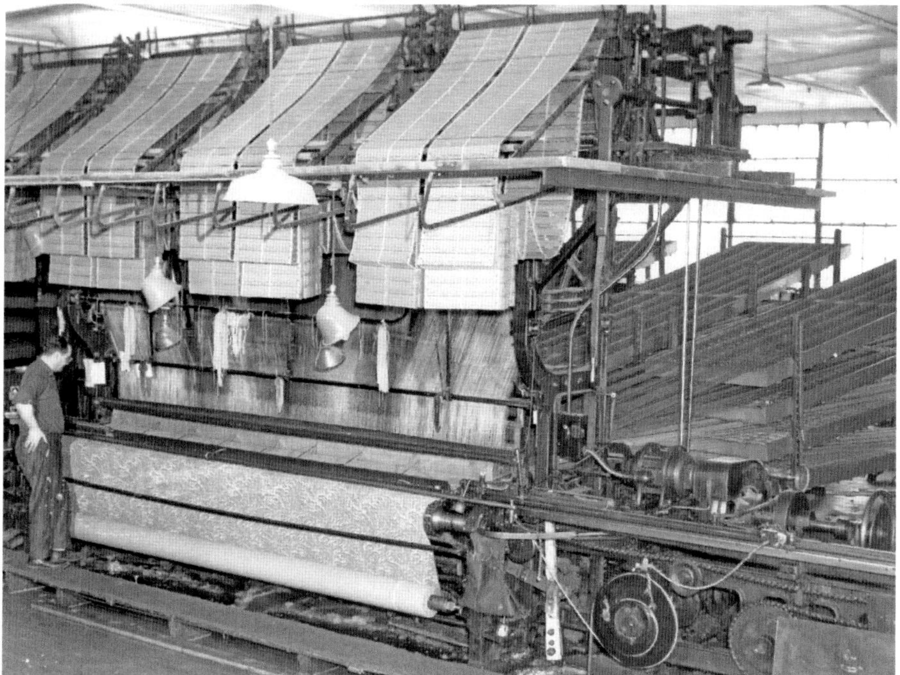

A Jacquard loom at Mohawk Mills with punch cards that controlled the carpet pattern. The system was a precursor of the computer. *Walter Elwood Museum.*

Wilton was a type of carpet woven at Mohawk using a system of paper punch cards invented by an eighteenth-century Frenchman named Joseph Jacquard. The punch card system was a precursor to the modern computer.

Silent Mike was a Wilton weaver, legendary in the East End for being a man of few words. My father, Clarence Cudmore, was also a Wilton weaver, as was Anthony Murdico, longtime boss of the local carpet workers union. My father and Domkowski sometimes were partners, which meant that one of them operated a given loom on the day shift and the other operated the same loom on the night shift. Weavers were paid on the piecework system. The more carpet they wove, the more money they made. Their yardage, though, had to pass muster with the finicky finishing room.

"Helen Burke, one of our sparehands, joined the WACCS," wrote the *Mohawker*. "You boys never met her but she tied a mean knot before she left." Sparehands and creelers tied hundreds of strong, yet small, "weaver's knots" to keep the looms running.

"I'm glad to hear that the Mill is well on its way producing blankets and tarpaulins," wrote U.S. Navy recruit Bruno Petruccione.

Both Mohawk and Bigelow-Sanford carpet mills in Amsterdam switched to making blankets and canvas during World War II, while their machine shops produced a variety of war-related products.

The lead story in the May 1943 newsletter reported that the War Department had presented the Army-Navy Production Award—the "E" pennant for excellence—to Mohawk. The company was the first carpet mill to deliver canvas to the war effort. Canvas was used for tents and to cover guns and other equipment.

"Canvas is sure a war commodity," wrote Louis McLaughlin from the USS *Jamestown*. "You would be surprised to see how much is used, even on the smaller ships. And of course, blankets are a necessity everywhere."

Wheel of Life

A few years before World War II, Mohawk Carpet Mills showed a flair for the dramatic and displayed artistic skill in making the *Wheel of Life*, perhaps the most spectacular carpet ever produced in Amsterdam. It took sixteen weavers eight months to create the Chenille carpet for the Waldorf Astoria Hotel on Park Avenue in New York City.

The center design depicts graphic and colorful scenes showing the progress of man from birth through death. The carpet was installed in 1938 and covered a mosaic depicting the same scenes designed by French artist Louis Rigal.

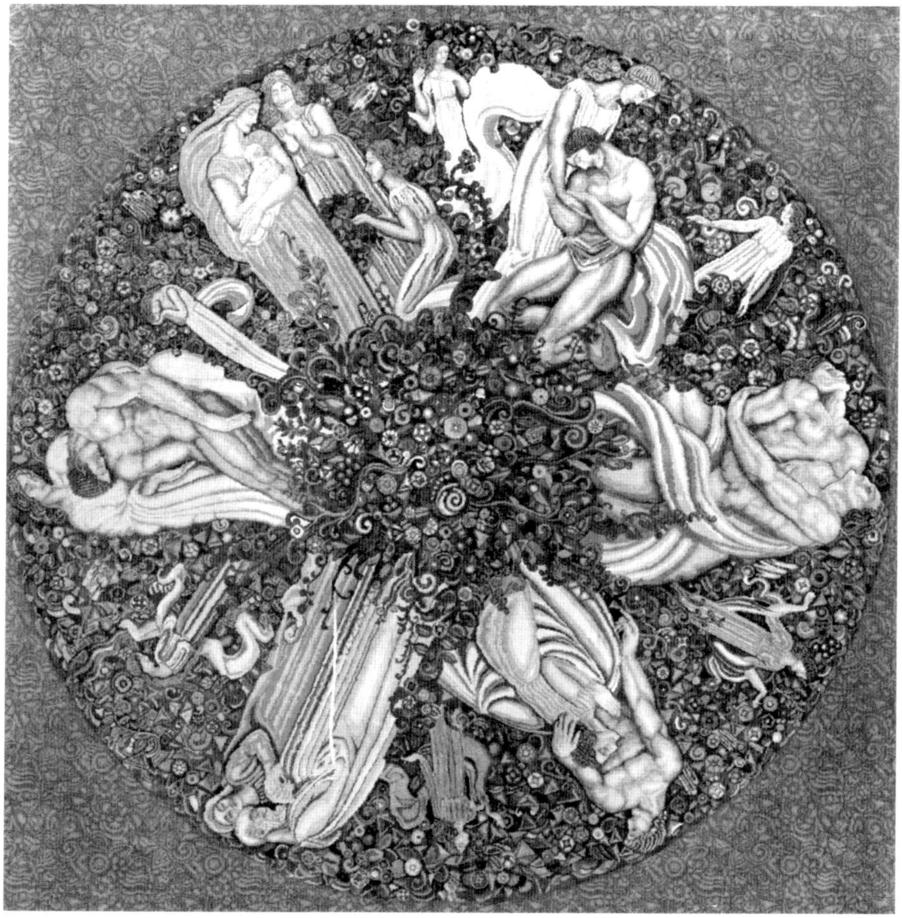

The center of the *Wheel of Life* carpet, woven in Amsterdam in 1938 for the Waldorf Astoria Hotel in New York City. *Walter Elwood Museum.*

The center design containing six picture groups was eighteen feet in diameter. The carpet weighed 850 pounds and was delivered to the hotel by a telephone pole trailer because of its size. It arrived in New York in the early morning to avoid traffic.

The carpet was removed several years later, uncovering the hotel's original Rigal mosaic. The mosaic is still there in the Waldorf Astoria's Park Avenue lobby.

After it left the hotel, the carpet went on tour. A 1946 newspaper ad promoted that a Spokane, Washington store was displaying the *Wheel of Life*. The ad said the carpet covered 333 square feet and used fifteen million wool tufts in sixty-nine colors.

Mohawk Mills displayed a large photo of the *Wheel of Life* at an industry convention in 1948 in Lake Placid. What happened to the carpet itself is not known. Today, color prints of the carpet are offered for sale online for over $300.

English Origin

Mohawk Mills traces its roots to the Shuttleworth family. William Shuttleworth and four sons came from England to America in 1875 and started a carpet mill in the Hudson Valley. After their father died, the four brothers moved to Amsterdam in 1878, taking over an empty factory building along the Mohawk River in the East End.

Mohawk Mills was created with the 1920 combination of the Shuttleworth Brothers mill and the McCleary, Wallin and Crouse rug factory, located in the city's Rockton section. That complex was known as the Upper Mill, and the East End location was called the Lower Mill. McCleary, Wallin and Crouse had learned the rug trade from Stephen Sanford.

Herbert L. Shuttleworth was named president of the merged company. His son Arthur succeeded him as head of Mohawk Mills starting in 1930, and another son, Howard, took the helm in 1940. Arthur's son, Herbert L. Shuttleworth II—who had spent some time running Amsterdam's New York Yankees farm team the Rugmakers—became Mohawk's executive vice-president in 1948. During World War II, Herbert served as a major in the U.S. Army quartermaster corps.

Postwar

As the Amsterdam mills went back to producing carpet after World War II, it appeared that the city's position as America's "Rug City" was solid.

The company magazine, *Tomohawk*, profiled a day in the life of a typical worker—electrician George Rink Jr.—in 1949. Rink's father had worked at the mill, as did George's five sisters at one time or another. George, his wife Cecilia and their children lived next door to his father on McCleary Avenue, within walking distance of the Upper Mill. The street was named for one of the original founders of that mill.

Rink had served four years in Europe in the U.S. Army. He was a sergeant and earned a Bronze Star and five battle stars.

One *Tomohawk* picture shows Rink, five-year old Carolyn and three-year old Donnie playing on the floor of their living room with the caption, "Like other young fathers who were separated from their families in the war, George spends lots of time with his children at home."

In 1949, Rink was a big and handsome man. He reminded me of the line drawings of the idealized factory worker that adorned the pages of the Textile Workers Union of America newsletter that came to our home.

That afternoon, Rink was putting in a new power line at the Chenille carpet department. At home after four, George found his father working in the garden.

Rink pitched a softball game that night. Pictured in their flashy uniforms were Rink and teammates "Gassy" Draus, "Flash" Coluni and John Brown.

Mohawk advertised extensively on the new medium of television and had a popular advertising jingle that was sung to the beat of a tom-tom: "Carpets from the looms of Mohawk; carpets for your rooms by Mohawk; rugs to grace your floors with beauty; woven for your roughest duty."

The Big Strike

Herbert Shuttleworth II became Mohawk Mills president in 1952. What workers called the "big strike" took place that year when members of the Textile Workers Union of America formed picket lines for twelve weeks at factories in northern cities, including Amsterdam.

"We got eleven cents [an hour raise]," said the late union leader Tony Murdico. "There were no ifs, ands or buts. We had to go back to work with 11 cents."

When Amsterdam celebrated its 150th anniversary in 1954, a huge parade marked the occasion. Ironically, one of the floats was a flying carpet. The next year, Bigelow-Sanford moved its carpet-making operation out of Amsterdam to Thompsonville, Connecticut.

Shuttleworth and Mohawk Mills made another kind of move: a 1955 merger with Alexander Smith, a carpet manufacturer in Yonkers, New York. The new company was called Mohasco.

For a while, management jobs from Alexander Smith helped boost Amsterdam's economy. But gradually, Mohasco moved manufacturing to southern states: the Carolinas and Georgia. Labor was cheaper there. Land and tax breaks were plentiful. By 1968, carpet manufacturing had ended in Amsterdam. Herbert Shuttleworth II retired in 1980. The last corporate offices left Amsterdam in 1987.

In 1992 and 1994, arson fires gutted the former Upper Mill complex at Forest Avenue and Lyon Street. The damaged buildings finally have been

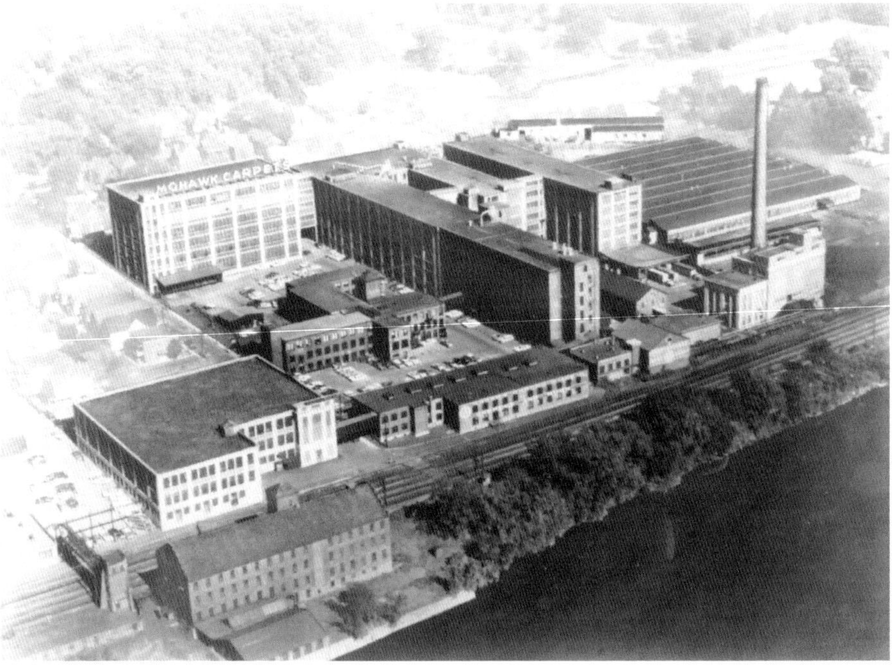

Mohasco Industries' Lower Mill in Amsterdam in 1962. *Walter Elwood Museum.*

torn down, and the site awaits development. Shuttleworth continued to make his home in Amsterdam and died in 2010 at age ninety-six. A few years before he died, the ballpark where his beloved Amsterdam Rugmakers used to play was renamed Herbert Shuttleworth II Park.

Tufting

Mark Thomann of Ackworth, Georgia, is the former director of historic preservation for Mohawk Industries, whose main office is in nearby Kennesaw.

Through the twists and turns of mergers in corporate America, since 1993 Mohawk Industries has been the descendant of both of Amsterdam's major carpet brands of the past: Mohasco/Mohawk Mills and Bigelow-Sanford.

One of the big reasons the carpet industry left Amsterdam and the Northeast, according to Thomann, was the invention of the tufting process to make carpets after World War II. Tufting produces carpet much more quickly than the weaving process used in Amsterdam. Thomann said that the tufting machines were too huge and heavy to fit into the old multistoried mill buildings in Amsterdam.

Although tufted carpets predominate today, some carpets are still woven the old-fashioned way at three locations: Eden, North Carolina; Landrum, South Carolina; and Bloomsburg, Pennsylvania.

Mohawk Industries has preserved over twenty thousand old carpet-pattern cards at its plant in Eden, North Carolina, to make it possible to re-create historic designs. Part of Thomann's job was to provide historically accurate carpets for theater renovations and other historic buildings. He provided such a carpet for the Fox Theatre in Atlanta, where *Gone with the Wind* premiered.

Underwear, Buttons and Strikes

Visitors to New York's Times Square a century ago saw the virtues of Amsterdam-made knit underwear up in lights. The Times Square sign was in place from 1912 to 1922. The company paid $3,000 a month for the sign, although the sign company wanted $6,000 a month.

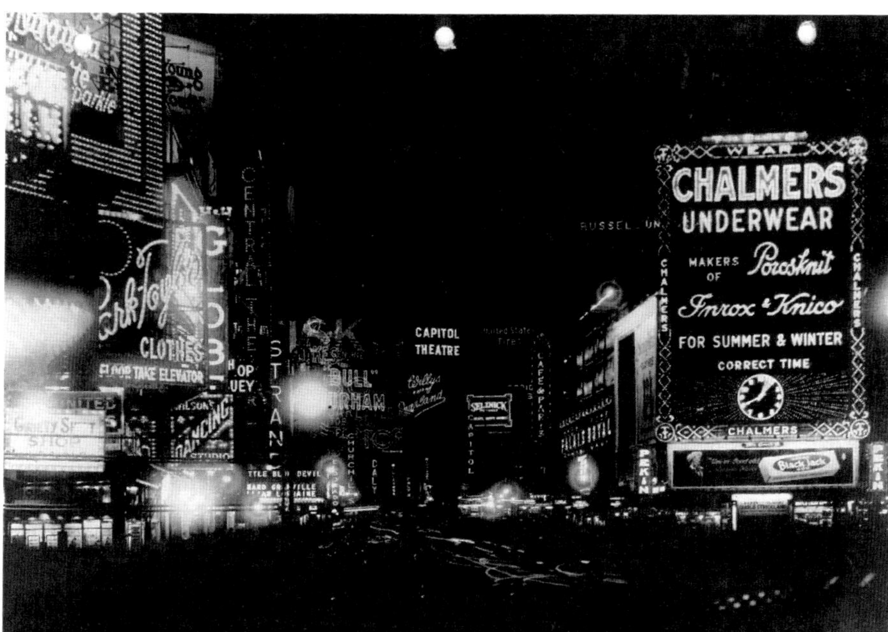

Chalmers underwear, made in Amsterdam, advertised in New York City's Time Square in the 1920s. *Joel Kaplan.*

Spelled out in electric lights on the sign was the following: "Chalmers underwear, makers ofOrosknit, Inrox and Kruco for summer and winter." A clock was below the sign.

According to historian Hugh Donlon, Amsterdam visitors never wearied of gawking at the sign. Certainly, the sign's prominent placement was a talking point for company salesmen, who could point out that the Amsterdam company was serious about national advertising.

David W. Chalmers and his partners were the last industrialists to start a major knitting mill in the city in 1901. In the next decade, Chalmers built his factory complex along the south shore of the Mohawk River.

Chalmers sold his mill in 1945 to Lester Martin and Company, which owned manufacturing plants in several cities. In 1946, Martin company controller Joel Kaplan began making trips to Amsterdam to inventory the Chalmers operation. In 1955, Kaplan moved to Amsterdam from New York City to oversee the Chalmers plant, which at one time during Martin's ownership employed 650 people. Martin died in 1959, and the Chalmers mill closed that same year.

In recent years, Long Island developer Uri Kaufman was unable to convince Amsterdam's Common Council to give him the opportunity to turn the long-vacant factory into apartments. The mill was slated for demolition in 2011.

Kaplan stayed in Amsterdam and became widely known for his service to more than twenty local charities. Kaplan has donated artifacts from Chalmers Knitting to the Walter Elwood Museum. Among them are advertisements for union suits—long cotton underwear for men that were Chalmers' main products in the old days. Kaplan said long underwear was popular before central heating and indoor plumbing.

Chalmers even made long underwear for summertime, according to a sales brochure: "Here's a 'keep cool' tip for hot weather days. Chalmers Porosknit underwear is knit to let the air circulate freely through the fabric. All perspiration is blotted up—no uncomfortable 'clinginess.' Porosknit 'lets the body breathe.'"

In the days when Lester Martin and Company owned Chalmers, the mill was mainly making ladies' and children's underwear and even handkerchiefs under the Fruit of the Loom label.

Chalmers Buttons

Donlon also noted that another family named Chalmers—Harvey and his son Arthur—started a button-manufacturing plant on the north side of the river in Amsterdam in 1898. The Chalmers button plant was built over the Chuctanunda Creek and produced thousands of buttons, originally using clamshells from the Mississippi River.

Donlon said, "Employment at peak output was about one thousand, including Amsterdam housewives, who added to family income by sewing buttons on cards at home." Buttons were so plentiful in Amsterdam that walkways at the Jollyland amusement park—now Shuttleworth Park—were paved with discarded buttons in the 1920s.

Labor Issues

Amsterdam knitting mills had ongoing labor problems, including what the *Morning Sentinel* newspaper called "the big lockout of 1886," which put thousands out of work for four months. The Knights of Labor initially walked out because a non-union spare hand was assigned spinners' work at the Schuyler and Blood mill. There were assaults and arrests. Knitting mill workers finally went back on the job in early 1887, amid "great excitement."

The Knights of Labor was the first labor union to admit women. Leonora Barry joined that union in Amsterdam in the 1880s. She worked in a mill sewing men's trousers for five cents a dozen. Barry left Amsterdam and went on to head the "women's department" in the Knights of Labor, resigning in 1889 amid criticism by some of her "high moral tone." Barry lived until 1930 and was popular on the lecture circuit as an advocate for temperance, suffrage and the rights of women in the workplace.

Rug City Was also Broom City

Amsterdam was among the first broom-making locations in New York because of broomcorn grown on islands and flats of the Mohawk River. In later years, the raw material came from western states. Broom making became such a significant part of the city's industrial heyday that the official seal of Amsterdam featured a carpet, a spool of thread and a couple of brooms.

James H. Bronson was operating a broom shop on Cedar Street employing about 175 hands in 1856. E.D. Bronson operated a similar shop on West Main Street. Historian Hugh Donlon noted that in the broom trade, factories were called "shops," regardless of size, and workers were "hands."

Other early broom makers were John D. Blood, who founded Amsterdam Broom & Brush Company in the 1860s, and Julius Wasserman, who started his Amsterdam Broom Company on Brookside Avenue in 1884.

The largest local shop was Pioneer Broom Company, founded by the Blood family in 1902 on Washington Street. A six-story factory was built in 1904 at West Main and Pine, plus a three-story annex on Cedar Street. Production continued until the 1930s. The buildings were later used by small textile firms.

Brothers William and Herbert Gardner worked for the Blood family and went out on their own in 1893. Their factory was on Chuctanunda Hill, a street running from Church to Grove on the east side of the Chuctanunda Creek. The Gardner Broom Company employed 250 hands in 1941 and was turning out nine thousand long-handled sweepers a day.

William Gardner was a two-term mayor of Amsterdam—in 1902 and again in 1930. Herbert Gardner was one of two Amsterdam industrialists to own a horse that won the Kentucky Derby.

A horse named George Smith, owned by Amsterdam carpet mill executive John Sanford, won the 1916 Kentucky Derby. Herbert Gardner owned 1929 Derby winner Clyde Van Dusen, named for the horse's trainer. After the Derby, Clyde Van Dusen—first male offspring of Man of War—never won another stakes race.

Amsterdam Broom Company

Julius Wasserman located his Amsterdam Broom Company in a three-story building on Brookside Avenue in 1884. Wasserman's son David joined the family business in 1889.

According to a publication from the 1930s called *Community Magazine*, Amsterdam Broom grew rapidly with Julius Wasserman handling manufacturing and with David running the office, purchasing raw materials and managing sales.

The firm employed 169 men in 1907, working a sixty-hour week, when fire broke out on April 9. The blaze was of unknown origin but was marked by "leaping flames and billowing smoke." A Brookside Avenue resident discovered the fire and turned in the alarm.

William Sullivan, an Eighth Ward Fire Company member, died when he was buried under a collapsing wall. The magazine reported that the city's limited firefighting capabilities could not save the main structure, although firefighters did rescue $70,000 in broomcorn. The Wassermans ordered coffee and sandwiches to be served through the night. Damage was estimated at $100,000.

The Wassermans decided to rebuild, moving offices temporarily to Main Street and making brooms in the former Globe Mill on Chuctanunda Hill until a new structure was built on Brookside Avenue.

In remarkably short order, a four-story building—with a sprinkler system—was constructed and opened in the fall of 1907. The Wassermans constructed an adjacent brick warehouse to store broomcorn.

Julius Wasserman died in 1916. During his lifetime, he also served as Amsterdam postmaster. Wasserman's company produced a number of highly regarded products, including the "Gold Bond" and "Brookside" brooms.

During the 1930s, the popularity of vacuum cleaners shrank the broom industry. When David Wasserman died in 1957, the factory building was put up for sale.

The Edy Brush Company of New York City purchased the structure and manufactured paint brushes, rollers and trays. Shawn K. Duffy, an Amsterdam native living near St. Louis, Missouri, worked at Edy Brush in the late 1960s. Duffy had to dye Polish hog bristles that arrived in large crates. Duffy also cut long tubes of synthetic bristles with a hand chopper until his arm practically fell off.

"I broke the elevator by loading boxes of bristle almost up to the limit of the elevator," Duffy wrote.

> *A co-worker and I were also told to stack boxes of bristle in a large storage room as high as we could. The ceiling was probably 30 to 40 feet. We made stairs out of the boxes as we stacked and therefore got right up to the ceiling. I don't think the foreman really expected this and we were in trouble again for doing what we were asked.*

Edy Brush closed in the early 1980s.

Eventually, the property was purchased by Thomas Eliopoulos, a developer and book dealer living in northern New Jersey. The building was renamed X-S Books Inc. and T.E. Enterprises.

The structure fell into disrepair and was vandalized. The city foreclosed in the spring of 2010 and was trying to get the owner to remove the books. The sprinkler system installed years ago by the Wassermans was not functioning when a massive blaze broke out in July 2010.

Two juveniles were accused of starting the fire that was fueled by thousands of books and a ruptured natural gas line. Charred pages from the books were carried by the wind and fell throughout Amsterdam. The fire destroyed the factory and a vacant home next door. The house across the street was left uninhabitable. At least five other homes sustained damage from heat thrown off by the blaze. About eighty people were evacuated, and twenty sought refuge in an American Red Cross shelter set up at Lynch Middle School.

The Family that Built Amsterdam

The family construction company founded by John J. Turner built Amsterdam's Clock Building, the former Elks Lodge on Division Street and schools including today's Lynch Literacy Academy. Skilled workers from the Turner firm spent four years renovating the mansion owned by the carpet-making Sanford family on Church Street, now city hall, and built many new homes for other captains of industry.

John J. Turner was born in 1853 in the town of Day, Saratoga County. He learned masonry and construction from his father, Michael Turner, an Irish immigrant. When Michael's wife, Bridget, died in 1872, he moved his family, including John, to Amsterdam, where they likely had relatives. Michael remarried and continued to work as a mason and builder.

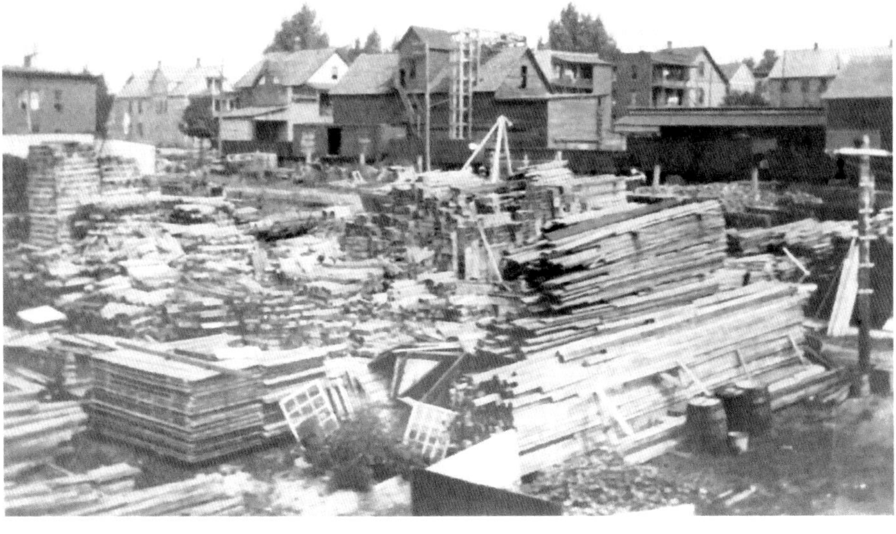

Turner Construction yard on Edward Street, Amsterdam. *Richard Gilston.*

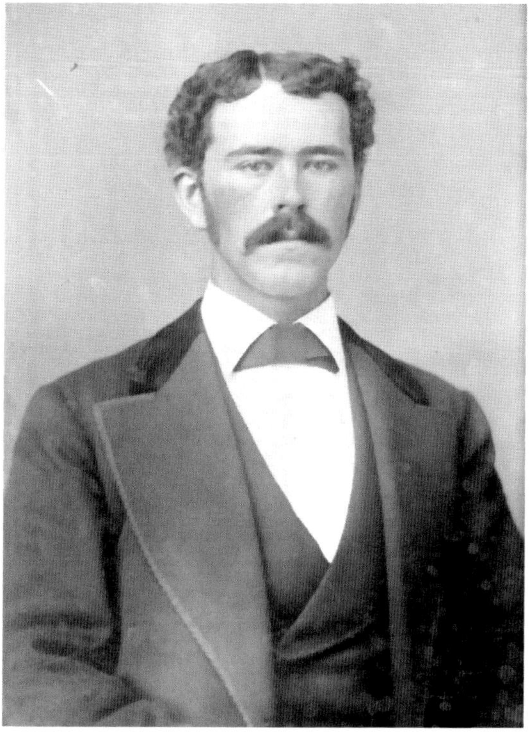

Builder John J. Turner's father, Michael, in 1865. Michael Turner drowned in the Mohawk River at Amsterdam in 1876. *Richard Gilston.*

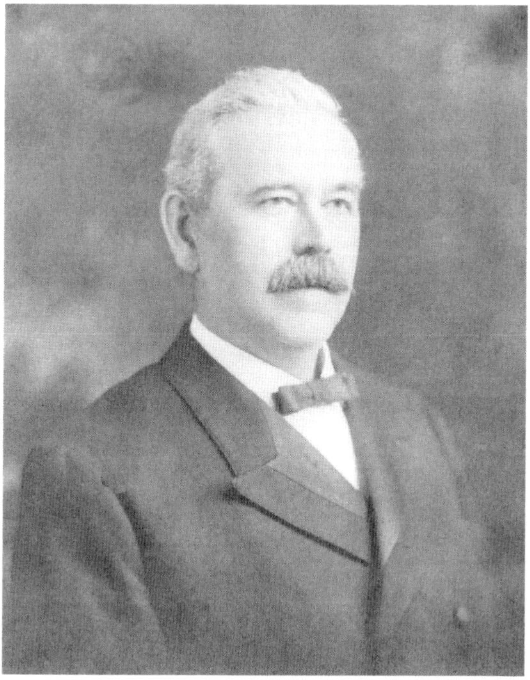

Amsterdam's master builder, John J. Turner, in 1916. *Richard Gilston.*

Tragedy struck the family on the night of April 24, 1876. Part of the existing bridge from Amsterdam to what was then Port Jackson had been destroyed by a spring ice floe. Michael Turner was the night watchman at a temporary ferry across the Mohawk River. About midnight, two attorneys who worked in Amsterdam engaged Michael to row them across the river to Port Jackson, where the men lived. Their small skiff overturned, and all three drowned.

John J. Turner found work in the building trades, at first with H.C. Grieme. When Amsterdam incorporated as a city in 1885, Turner was elected to the board of aldermen as a Democrat.

He partnered with others building important structures in the Amsterdam area and even helped build the state prison in Dannemora in northern New York. In business for himself after 1902, he erected the trolley car power station in Tribes Hill and a number of buildings for General Electric in Schenectady and Pittsfield, Massachusetts.

John Turner and Sons went into business as a construction company about 1906. All three sons of John and Maria Egan Turner were educated in civil engineering at Rensselaer Polytechnic Institute in Troy.

Renovation of Amsterdam's Sanford mansion, starting in 1913, was said to be John J. Turner's proudest achievement. Although he worked on the mansions of others, Turner lived in a modest brick home at 53 Union Street. He died in 1924 at age seventy-one.

His eldest son and then company president John P. Turner died three years later of a heart attack at age forty-five. John P. Turner had supervised completion of the power station opposite Cranesville, now Cranesville Block, and was especially proud of building the then-new St. Mary's Hospital in Amsterdam.

Richard E. Turner, who was deaf, then headed the firm until his death in 1940 at age fifty-six. He was owner of the Amsterdam Rugmakers baseball team and an accomplished photographer. Richard and his brother, Thomas A. Turner, are credited with building Lynch school, the Century Club and other Amsterdam landmarks, plus the Gideon Putnam Hotel in Saratoga Springs.

After the start of World War II, the business went into decline. Thomas A. Turner remained active in local civic affairs until his death in 1953 at age sixty-five.

Dr. Richard R. Gilston, great-grandson of John J. Turner, compiled the information used in this story. Gilston is a physician in Greenland, New Hampshire. Brothers Richard, John, Bob and Eric Gilston collaborated on a segment on Turner Construction that was part of WMHT-TV's *Our Town Amsterdam* documentary in 2010.

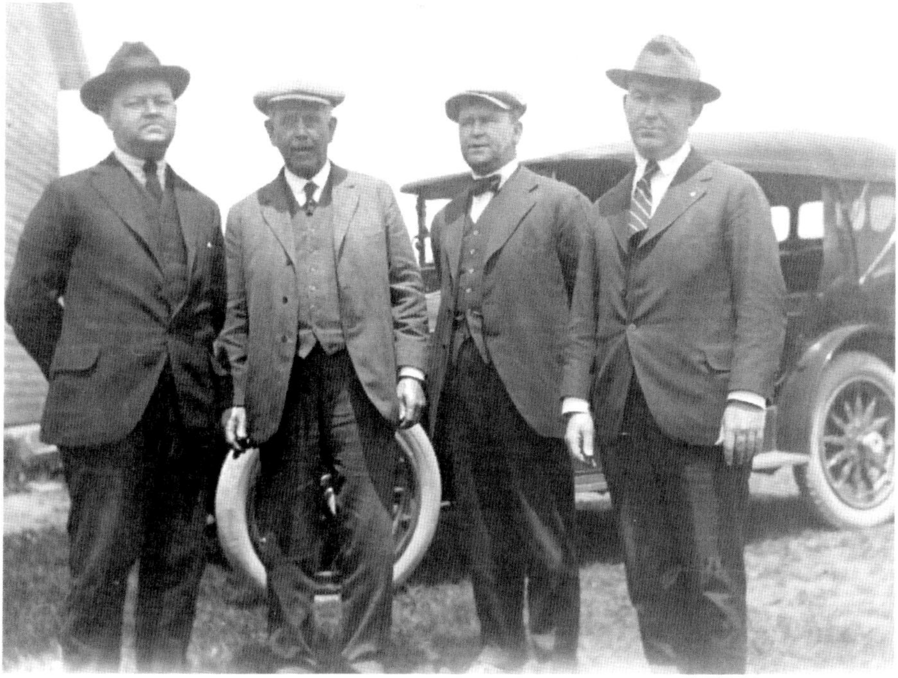

John J. Turner and Sons in 1920. *Left to right*: Richard E., John J., John P. and Thomas A. Turner. *Richard Gilston.*

Richard Gilston wrote:

> *Through their own hard work, ingenuity, and competitiveness the Turner family built much of the physical backbone of the developing city of Amsterdam including mills, dams, financial institutions, hospitals, schools, social clubs and homes for the newly wealthy and the not so wealthy.*
>
> *Throughout they remained good citizens contributing to the social and cultural fabric of their community. In the process they raised their own families and countless other immigrants out of poverty and put them within reach of achieving their own American dreams.*

Deindustrialization, the End of an Era

In 1992 and again in 1994, fire gutted most of the former Mohasco complex, called the Upper Mill, at Forest Avenue and Lyon Street in Amsterdam.

The late Tony Murdico, who had been union president at Mohasco, was devastated:

> *Well I felt bad. Especially I felt bad when Number One Mill was burning and I worked in Number One Mill. And when that came down I was across the street and I spent a lot of time, a lot of years in there you know. My feeling was something out of this world. You just can't believe a big place like this burned down.*

Murdico was born in Reggio Calabria in the south of Italy and came to Amsterdam with his family when he was eight years old. He lied about his age to get a job at Mohawk Carpet when he was only fourteen in 1929.

Murdico said:

> *We came right into Amsterdam from Italy and we thought it was beautiful, you know. We were picking olives in Italy to make a living. And we came here and we thought it was another, a different world. When I became president of the union it was the best thing that could happen to me—a foreigner coming over from Italy.*

Anthropologist Studies Amsterdam

During the time of the Mohasco fires, from 1992 to 1994, a University at Albany anthropology graduate student lived in Amsterdam and wrote her doctoral dissertation on the city's industrial decline.

Susan R. Dauria, now chairperson of the department of anthropology at Bloomsburg University in Pennsylvania, thought that one way to understand life in a mill town was to get a job on an assembly line. She worked at Hasbro, a toymaker then located in Amsterdam.

Dauria said the assembly line was tough: "I think the hardest thing was you had to keep up with the machine. Every thirty seconds that thing would make a mold and you had to keep up with that."

According to Dauria, Amsterdam experienced two periods of deindustrialization. The major blow was the flight of the carpet mills to the South in the 1950s and 1960s as the industry sought cheaper, non-union labor and more room to install new carpet-making technology. Amsterdam experienced another economic blow in the 1980s, when Coleco, a toymaker that had taken over former carpet mill buildings, "made bad investment decisions after the success of the Cabbage Patch doll."

The city's Polish, Italian and other European immigrants were drawn to Amsterdam by the prospering carpet industry from the turn of the century through the 1920s. Latino immigration took off in the 1950s as the carpet mills were departing and the city's overall population was declining. Initially, Latinos worked in low-paying, marginal industries that were established in Amsterdam to take advantage of government incentives aimed at helping the struggling local economy. Some mills in New York City with a Puerto Rican workforce, for example, relocated to Amsterdam. A second group of Latinos, Dauria wrote, came to Amsterdam seeking *tranquilidad*—refuge from the crime, drugs and violence in New York City.

In her thesis, Dauria argued that the upward mobility of the carpet industry helped European immigrants assimilate into American life in the first half of the twentieth century. However, "reduced economic opportunity" in the second half of the twentieth century, she said, played a significant role in increasing the importance of ethnic allegiance for Latinos, especially Latina women.

Until the 1950s, Amsterdam was a company town, Dauria said, in which every third person was employed in the carpet industry.

She continued:

> *People that moved here in the early 1900s to work for the carpet mills did very well and they sent their children to college. They talk about the toil and the struggle, and there was a lot of that. The toil and struggle brought them prosperity eventually. It's a success story and a really sad story when you finally hear that by 1968 no carpets are being made in Amsterdam. It was gone. But that's a story that you can hear in other towns, too, in the U.S.*

Dauria found that people in Amsterdam were "pretty generous" in not blaming the carpet industry for leaving town: "They kind of say, well, this is a capitalist market. In order for the company to survive, they had to move on."

She found that local people were angrier over the performance of Coleco, which came to Amsterdam in 1968. The company boomed in 1983 with the Cabbage Patch doll, only to face bankruptcy in 1988 with the ill-fated production of the Adam computer.

Dauria has also described how older European immigrants and newer Latino immigrants have clashed: "The generation that came here earlier, they're much older now and they have a different outlook about what it is to be an American and what it is to be successful. This latest group has a very different reality."

She added, "They all want the same thing. It's really ironic. Everybody wants a nice place to live, a little bit of economic security."

Dauria found that Amsterdam still maintains a small-town feeling and that the people she met in the early 1990s were key to that pleasant ambience.

"I am indebted to this community," Dauria said.

> *My dissertation wouldn't have been successful if it weren't for people talking with me. For example, sometimes I would meet someone through a contact of a contact of a contact, and I would talk with them, and they would tell me their whole life story. So I had a really nice experience there. I miss it on some level. I miss Amsterdam. So you know, even though people can be critical of it, as an insider I had a nice—a very nice—experience.*

Dauria's doctoral dissertation is called "Deindustrialization and the Construction of History and Ethnic Identity: The Case of Amsterdam, New York." There are copies in the Amsterdam and New York State libraries and at the Department of Anthropology at SUNY Albany.

URBAN RENEWAL

Hugh Donlon's 1980 *Annals of a Mill Town* gives an account of the history of urban renewal in Amsterdam, which Donlon said involved three somewhat coordinated efforts: arterialization, or new highways; urban renewal itself, marked primarily by the downtown mall; and construction of public housing, mainly on Division Street.

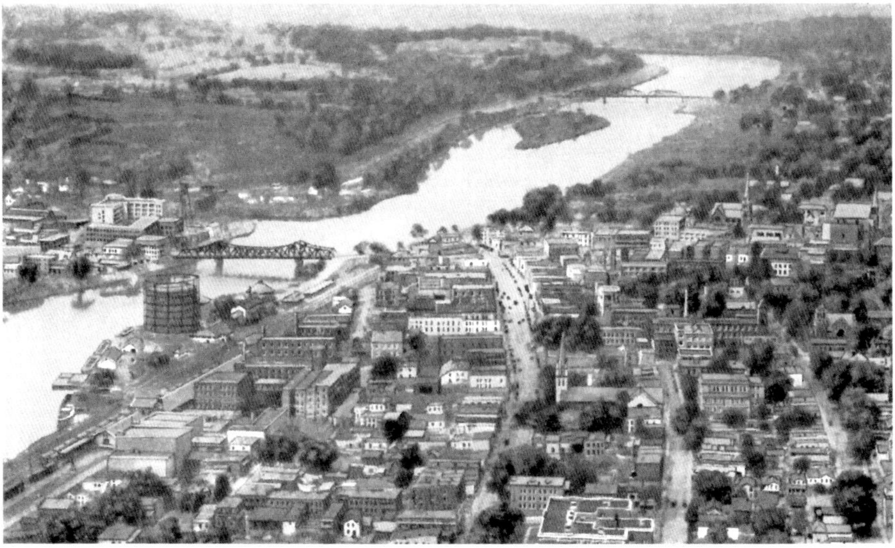

Aerial view of Amsterdam before urban renewal. *Gerald B. Snyder.*

The first highway modernization was Route 5S on the South Side, which was relocated in 1956 from the former Bridge Street business district to its current location on higher ground near the New York State Thruway that opened in 1954. By 1960, the four-lane Route 30 stretch from the Thruway to the Mohawk River had been created, with demolition of thirty buildings. Route 30 on the North Side from the river to the top of Market Hill was not completed until 1968.

The current Mohawk River bridge cost over $7 million, took four years to build and was completed in 1973. The old bridge was torn down a year later.

The four-lane section of Route 5 north and east of the old bridge was under construction at the same time as the new bridge, although demolition of sixty buildings for the project began in 1966.

Transportation changes continued until 1979, including relocation of the West End railroad tracks and creation of another western stretch of four-lane highway for Route 5.

Amsterdam's highways continue to confuse out-of-towners and even locals. "Many arterial [highway] navigators flunked first tests of arterial sign reading from clustered overhead directives," Donlon wrote.

Creation of the downtown mall, today the Riverfront Center, began in 1973. In a move deplored by many, the mall was built so that it blocked Main Street, dividing the city. Some called it the Berlin Mall. The first section of the downtown mall was opened in 1977, although work continued on the complex into the 1980s.

About four hundred buildings, one hundred of them from the nineteenth century, were demolished in the city for urban renewal, primarily in the formerly dense downtown.

Fort Johnson Changes

The village of Fort Johnson also changed drastically in the early 1960s, when 2.26 miles of two-lane Route 5 were converted into a four-lane limited access highway. The cost estimate for the Fort Johnson project was $1.88 million.

The 5.72-mile Tribes Hill Route 5 project to the west was estimated at $1.64 million. The new road skirted Tribes Hill, and relatively few buildings were destroyed. The road project eliminated many curves and narrow stretches that had caused accidents over the years.

Newspaper clippings from a collection kept by the late Francis Dodds of Amsterdam show vanished Fort Johnson landmarks. Dodds's parents' home in Fort Johnson was one of the houses taken.

Contractor Henry Butler tore down thirty-five homes and twenty other structures in Fort Johnson, most of them on the south side of old Route 5.

An Atlantic auto service station, fuel tanks and the popular Tollner's ice cream stand on Route 5 were among the first buildings torn down.

Old Fort Johnson itself, built in 1749, was spared. However, an imposing stone wall and stately walnut trees in front of the historic building were torn down for the new highway.

West of the Old Fort, another business that was demolished was Mohawk Lodge, a long-established eating and drinking establishment, operated in its last years by Harold Philip and his wife.

Lepper Creek, near the city of Amsterdam, and Kayaderosseras Creek, near Old Fort Johnson, were routed underneath the new Route 5 by way of new culverts.

The People of the Valley

Amsterdam's Psychedelic Philosopher

Over one hundred years ago, a philosopher and poet living in Amsterdam experimented with mind-altering drugs to have mystical experiences.

Benjamin Paul Blood had been given nitrous oxide (laughing gas) during a dental operation in 1860. According to Blood, the gas "opened his mind to new ideas." He continued experimenting with it.

In 1874, Blood published a pamphlet called *The Anesthetic Revelation and the Gist of Philosophy*. The great American philosopher William James reviewed the pamphlet for the *Atlantic* magazine, and James, too, began using nitrous oxide to have mystical experiences.

Blood sent his pamphlet far and wide, and according to a 1996 article in the *Atlantic* by Dmitri Tymoczko, "a tiny group of nitrous oxide philosophers" formed in America and England, using the drug to create "some sort of incommunicable metaphysical illumination."

Of the mystical condition, Blood wrote, "Although it may have been attained otherwise, I know [it] by the use of anesthetic agents."

Tymoczko said that the empirical James was attracted to Blood's chemically induced mysticism because it lacked religious content. They called their concept "pluralism," meaning that mystic experiences could be religious, drug-induced or achieved by other means. One might say that Blood and James, not Ken Kesey and Timothy Leary, started America's first psychedelic movement.

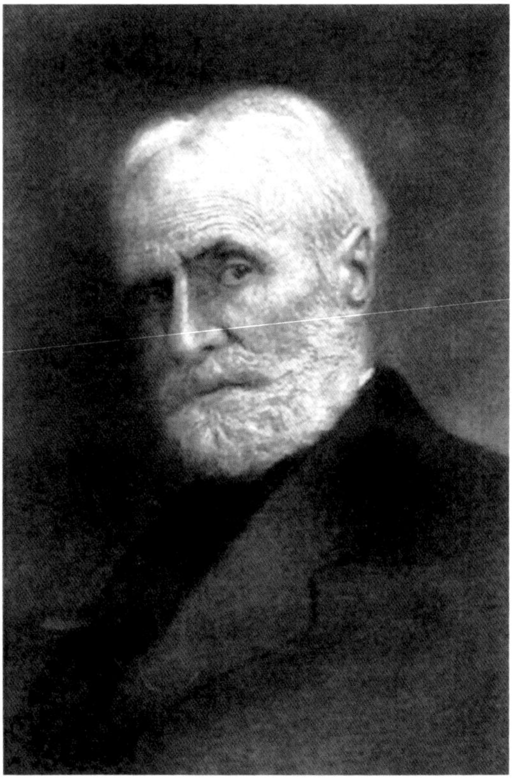

Amsterdam poet and philosopher Benjamin Paul Blood. *From Blood's book* Pluriverse.

"Mr. Blood inhabits a city otherwise, I imagine, quite unvisited by the Muses, the town called Amsterdam, situated on the New York Central Railroad," wrote James in an essay called "The Pluralistic Mystic."

> *What his regular or bread-winning occupation may be I know not, but it can't have made him super-wealthy. He is an author only when the fit strikes him, and for short spurts at a time; shy, moreover, to the point of publishing his compositions only as private tracts, or in letters to such far-from-reverberant organs of publicity as the* Gazette *or the* Recorder *of his native Amsterdam.*

"Blood could multiply large numbers in his head," wrote Tymoczko. "He could demolish the itinerant lecturers who were a staple of nineteenth-century American popular culture. On one occasion he demonstrated to an astonished crowd how a visiting spiritualist had produced apparently ghostly occurrences."

Shortly before he died in 1910, James closed a letter to his Amsterdam friend with the phrase "Warm regards, fellow pluralist!" James had just written his last published work, an article about Blood for that July's *Hibbert Journal*, a liberal Christian periodical published in England.

"Signed by me, but written mainly by yourself," wrote James to Blood. James included a lengthy quote from Blood's essay on progress.

Blood wrote, "We have dreamed of a climax and consummation, a final triumph where a world shall burn in barbecue; but there is not, cannot be a purpose of eternity; it shall pay mainly as it goes or not at all."

In addition to his friendship with William James, Blood also corresponded with the British poet Alfred Lord Tennyson.

Born in 1832 near Fort Johnson, Blood was the only son of John and Mary Stanton Blood, who owned seven hundred acres of land on both sides of the Mohawk River. Benjamin Paul grew up in a large brick house on the family farm in the town of Florida, on the south shore of the Mohawk River. He was educated at Amsterdam Academy and studied for a time at Union College in Schenectady.

Blood made a living as a farmer but became well known locally for writing poems and letters to the editor and for studying philosophy. In a letter to James, Blood said, "I do farming in a way, but am much idle. I have been a sort of pet of the city, and think I should be missed. In a large vote taken by one of the daily papers here a month or so ago as to who were the twelve leading citizens, I was sixth in the twelve."

Blood's letters to area newspapers sometimes dealt with local politics or the tricks of spiritualist mediums. He also wrote on the principles of industry, finance and metaphysics. His poetry included titles such as "The Bride of the Iconoclast," "Justice" and "Optimism."

He was married to Mary Sayles, and after her death he married Harriet Lefferts. He had a daughter from each marriage and a son.

Blood died on January 15, 1919, after a two-week illness that was reported as the first serious sickness of his life. He was living at 10 Eagle Street. His funeral took place at the home of his daughter, Mrs. Francis Morris, on Guy Park Avenue.

His obituary said Blood was "one of the most striking personalities ever to live in Amsterdam." A strong man in his youth, the obituary reported that Blood was a "stately, commanding figure" when he walked city streets. He was buried at Green Hill Cemetery.

A *Recorder* editorial after Blood died praised him for having a powerful body and a mind "high above the common." The editorial continued, "So far did he go in philosophic thought in his public writings that most of his readers could not follow him."

Blood was working on a book at the time of his death. *Pluriverse: An Essay in the Philosophy of Pluralism* was printed posthumously by his literary executor, Horace Kallen. In a foreword, Kallen remarks how it was unusual to find a mystic like Blood living in a "dingy" city such as Amsterdam. Kallen also was editor of William James's unfinished works and a co-founder of the New School for Social Research. Kallen donated Blood's papers to Harvard's Houghton Library in 1955.

Blood's *Pluriverse* has been digitized as part of Google's print library project. The book has chapters on fairly inscrutable topics such as duplexity, idealism and cause, plus a chapter on Jesus and free will.

The book ends with a plea for knowledge. "Knowing is the soul's all," wrote Blood. He calls for his epitaph to be "Greeting, if thou hast known."

Scribner's magazine printed Blood's last poem, "Resurgere," shortly before his death:

Though shrapnel-stripped, the poplars rear
Bare fingers to the shivering skies,
Some leaves will come another year
To whisper that the dead will rise.

Queen Libby of Fonda

People in Fonda called her Queen Libby. A formidable woman from Italy, Queen Libby stopped a train, saved a man from the electric chair and became a major property owner in Fonda.

Elizabeth Luciano was born in Pietremalara, near Naples, Italy, in 1872. She came to America alone when she was fifteen and settled in Fonda to be near relatives who lived in Johnstown. She married another Italian immigrant, James Cassell. They had three children before Cassell died at the age of thirty-three. Libby then married Alfonso Mancini, who worked for the railroad, and had four more children. For a time, Libby and Alfonso returned to Italy, where Alfonso was a jailor. Libby returned to America by herself, and Alfonso eventually followed her.

According to one of her grandchildren, Libby was a large woman who received her nickname when she knocked down a man who had used an ethnic slur about Italians. "The next time you see me, you bow," Libby told the fallen man, leading him to refer to her as "Queen Libby" or "Queen Lib."

Queen Libby ran a boardinghouse and grocery store in the west end of Fonda, where she fed, housed and cared for Italian immigrants who worked on the railroad. She had a good head for business and purchased sixteen two-family houses in the village. Patsy Cassell, one of Libby's sons, ran a popular Fonda tavern called Patsy's for many years.

In 1923, one of Libby's daughters, Eva Mancini Pepe, was about to give birth to her first child. Eva had married Ralph Pepe, whose father, Salvatore, had founded Pepe's Bakery, a family business on Amsterdam's South Side that continued operations into the twenty-first century.

According to the *Recorder* from January 20, 1923, Libby was informed by telephone that her daughter was about to have a rare Caesarean section at St. Mary's Hospital in Amsterdam.

Libby secured a red flag at the Fonda train station, and when an express came "thundering in its usual way," she waved the red flag, convincing the engineer to stop the train and then convincing him to take her to Amsterdam. Arriving at the hospital, she charged into the operating room.

Libby also made a phone call to the New York Central Railroad and demanded that the next possible train stop in Fonda to take her husband to Amsterdam.

The headline from the newspaper clipping reads: "Flags train to reach daughter as stork comes: Fonda woman bossed the whole New York Central Railroad but got to Amsterdam hospital on time."

The child born that day was Vincenza Pepe, who passed away in 2001. Eva Pepe had seven children, and the child she bore in 1924 was Salvatore Pepe of Amsterdam, who provided information for this story.

"Queen Libby was strong-minded, tough, but a gentle grandmother," Pepe said, recalling that Libby gave quarters to her grandchildren.

Ann Nardick Sherman of Amsterdam also claims Queen Libby as a grandmother. Sherman's mother was Constance Cassell, one of the children from Libby's first marriage.

According to Sherman, Libby was an interpreter for Italians who could not speak English and were brought before the court in Fonda, the county seat. Libby once saved an innocent man from the electric chair. Libby called Italy, where the real murderer had fled, and had him sent back to the United States for trial. Governor Franklin Roosevelt was so impressed that he visited Fonda to commend Libby, and a parade was held in her honor.

Queen Libby died in 1938, and her grandchildren say her funeral was the biggest funeral ever seen in Fonda.

AFRICAN AMERICAN HISTORY

The Montgomery County Heritage and Genealogical Society has installed a state historical marker outside the 131 Mohawk Street home where Chester "Bromley" Hoke lived in Canajoharie.

Hoke was born in 1847. Not much is known about his parents, but his grandparents were slaves. His grandfather, Henry Miller, was owned by John Miller from Minden. His grandmother was owned by Adam Garlock of Canajoharie. Hoke's grandparents presumably were freed when New York abolished slavery on July 4, 1827.

At age sixteen, Hoke volunteered to serve in the Fifty-fourth Massachusetts Regiment, one of the first African American units in the Civil War. The regiment was the subject of the 1989 movie *Glory*. Hoke returned to Canajoharie after the war and was a porter at the Nellis Hotel. He had four sons with his wife, Elizabeth Phillips. He had previously had a daughter. According to his 1913 obituary, Hoke was a good baseball player, as were some of his Canajoharie descendants.

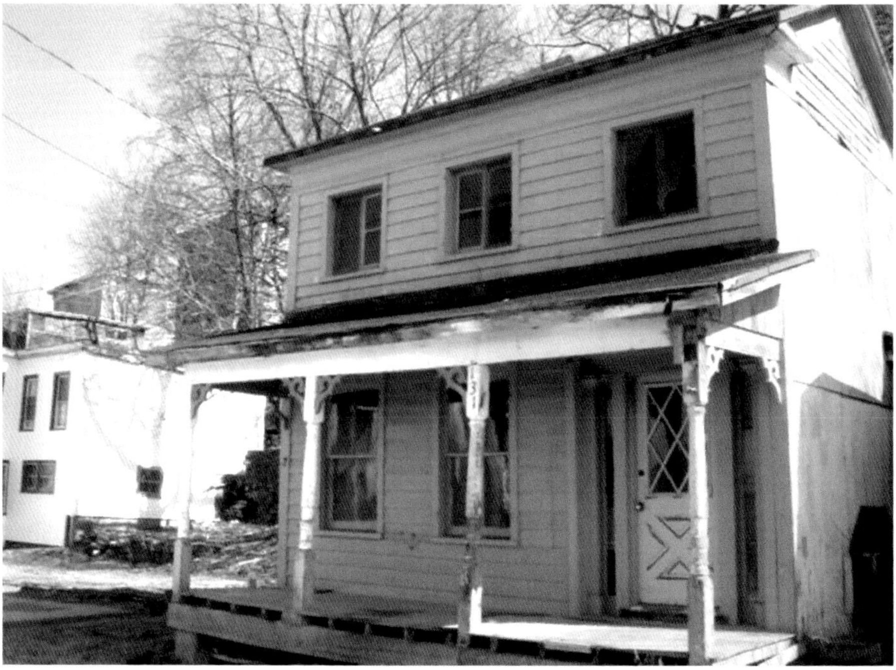

Chester "Bromley" Hoke's Canajoharie home today. *Kelly Farquhar.*

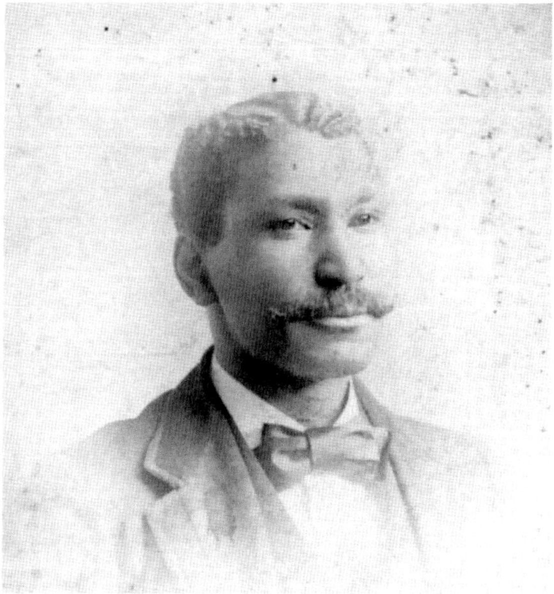

Chester "Bromley" Hoke of Canajoharie. *New York State Museum, Albany.*

Amsterdam figures in the story of a decorated black Civil War soldier. A native of Oswego County, Bruce Anderson received one of the last Medals of Honor from the war. Anderson and twelve others of the 142nd New York Infantry cut down a palisade blocking the advance of Union forces in an attack on Fort Fisher in North Carolina in 1865. They were recommended for the medal, but the paperwork was lost. Anderson hired a lawyer and finally received the medal in 1914. He spent the last years of his life in Amsterdam, died in 1922 and is buried in Green Hill Cemetery.

Montgomery County historian Kelly Farquhar has assembled a team to gather information on African Americans who lived in the county from 1820 to 1880. The black population grew in that period, perhaps because of the abolition of slavery at an early date in New York. Farquhar said blacks were concentrated in small villages like Fonda and Canajoharie. Local black families included the Hokes, Jacksons, Bloods, Wilsons and McKinneys. After 1880, local blacks apparently sought more opportunity in bigger cities.

Farquhar's work is being funded by local sources and $10,000 from Preserve New York, a grant program of the Preservation League of New York State and the New York Council on the Arts. Farquhar, SUNY Oswego professor emeritus Judith Wellman and local historians Scott Haefner and Alessa Wylie also will document the local abolition movement and survey sites related to the Underground Railroad. They hope to complete the project in 2012.

The Underground Railroad was a network of safe structures and people who helped runaway slaves flee to Canada. Even after New York abolished slavery, escaped slaves were still considered stolen property in the state, in

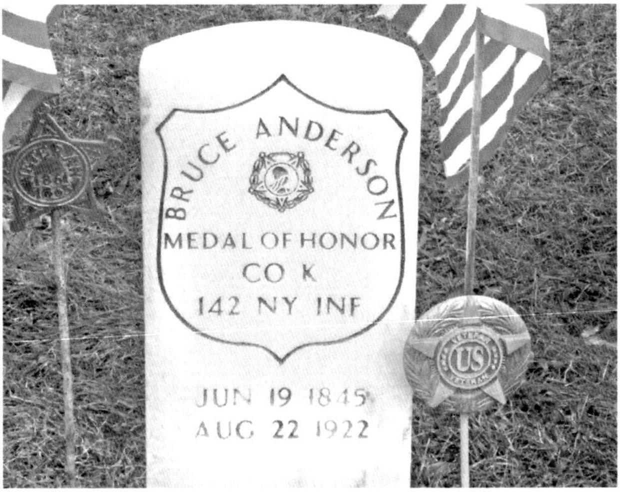

Tombstone of Bruce Anderson, Green Hill Cemetery, Amsterdam. *Alessa Wylie.*

effect stealing themselves from their masters when they ran away. Anyone caught harboring an escaped slave was subject to arrest.

"When you think of the Underground Railroad, legendary figures such as Harriet Tubman, Frederick Douglass, Gerrit Smith and John Brown come to mind," Farquhar said. "But local families like the Clizbes, Hagamans, Swarthouts, Hartleys, Voorhees and Freys, to name a few, were involved in the movement as well."

Ellis Clizbe of Amsterdam is known to have paid for escaped slaves or sheltered them. According to an 1855 account, Clizbe lived between two black families.

A barn at Freysbush Church on Route 163 in Minden may have been a hiding place for the runaways. Ames, south of Canajoharie, could have been a stop on the Underground Railroad, along with what are now two bed-and-breakfasts—the Inn by the Mill in St. Johnsville and Halcyon Farm in Florida.

The recollections of Elizabeth Jones McFee of Ames have been recorded; she tells of going with either her father or grandfather to transport a freedom seeker hidden in a stove to the home of Dr. Mereness, the next safehouse. One man who likely was part of the Underground Railroad was Reverend Richard Eastep of the African Methodist Episcopal Church in Canajoharie. An 1857 letter makes reference to Eastep sheltering fugitive slaves.

Farquhar said the abolition movement also involved antislavery conventions, church rallies and financial support.

Fritz Vogt—Homeless Man Who Chronicled Home Life

Fritz Vogt slept in barns and relieved the pain of rheumatism with too much alcohol. He spoke broken English and died at a poorhouse. And he left a collection of two hundred drawings that became the subject of an exhibition at the American Folk Art Museum in New York City in 2003.

"No one knows what Fritz Vogt did during the first forty-eight years of his life in Germany, where he was born in 1841," wrote *New York Times* reviewer Ken Johnson. In 1890, Vogt came to America and spent his last ten years as a traveling artist, recording what Johnson called "lucid descriptions" of the homes of his clients, primarily farmers in Schoharie and Montgomery Counties. He did forty drawings of farms, churches and other buildings in the town of Sharon, for example, and twenty-five in Canajoharie. He died in the poorhouse of the town of Palatine in 1900.

The late W. Parker Hayes Jr., a project director for the Smithsonian Institution's traveling exhibition service, produced the catalogue book for Vogt's retrospective: *Drawn Home: Fritz Vogt's Rural America*. The catalogue was published by the Fenimore Art Museum in Cooperstown, New York. The Arkell Museum in Canajoharie has also displayed Vogt's work.

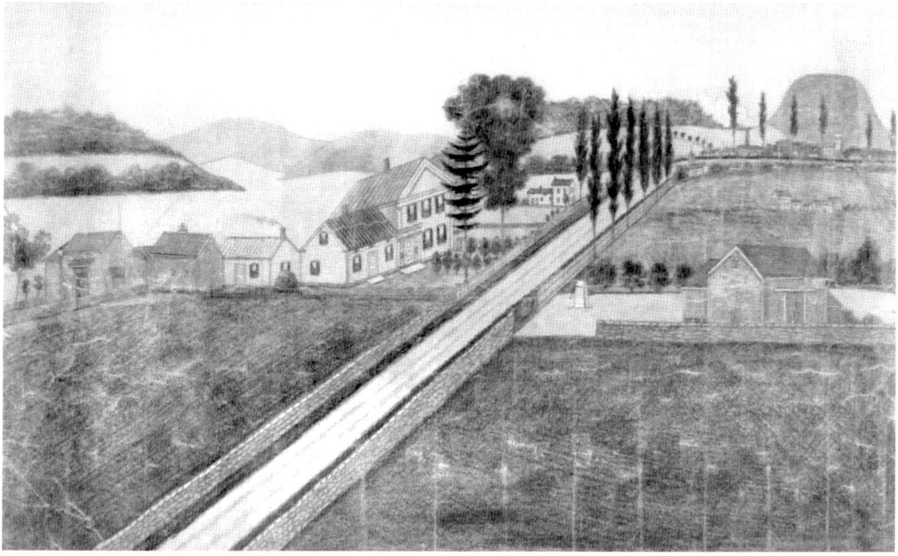

The Old Brown Homestead, Carlisle, N.Y., by Fritz Vogt, 1898. *Fenimore Art Museum, Cooperstown, New York.*

At first, Vogt drew realistically with graphite pencils. He then switched to colored pencils, and his work became more complex with multiple perspectives.

"Somebody could have happened to buy him a set of colored pencils," Hayes said. "Or somebody said 'I want this in color,' and all of a sudden his constituency decided, 'Hey I want my work in color.'"

Why did farmers want pictures of their homes? Hayes said New York State agriculture was facing competition from the Midwest. There was nostalgia for the dwindling numbers of "gentleman farmers." Vogt's drawings also mirror another late nineteenth-century social trend: publication of county atlases depicting the homes of wealthy people. Hayes was able to chronicle Vogt's life from oral histories recorded in the 1960s, interviews with elderly people who had known Vogt when they were children. Hayes created a database of Vogt's work to fill in biographical details, as the artist dated and described each drawing.

The oral histories, for example, state that Vogt picked hops. "In August of every year from 1891 until he died, he didn't do any drawings," Hayes said. "August is the beginning of the hops-picking season. You can prove or verify what's out there about Fritz Vogt through what the drawings say."

A few drawings indicate that Vogt was paid a couple of dollars for a specific piece. Vogt was more often paid in kind, with a place to stay, meals or alcohol.

Vogt fit in with the region's existing German American population. "He relied on an ethnic network to get the basic things in life and to find patrons," Hayes said. Vogt had a "good rapport" with children and may have earned money by teaching German.

Hayes wrote that Vogt was "a short, smallish man with a quick step, yet slightly rotund." He added:

> *He wore five or six secondhand shirts layered over each other, the underlying shirts visible through holes in the outer layers. He slept in the shelter of barns between two buffalo hides on a pile of hay. When Vogt entered a home to complete his drawings, he wore a pair of slippers or crude shoes fashioned from carpet remnants.*

"There often are little things in his drawings," Hayes said. "The way a certain cornice has some flourish. He saw those things. He knew the homeowners who lived there were very attuned to that. But at the same time he had a perspective that was different because he didn't have a home."

Hayes wrote, "We are left with the great irony of a homeless man who expressed an intimate knowledge of the idea of home."

Kirk Douglas

One of the world's oldest celebrity bloggers is a native of Amsterdam. Actor and producer Kirk Douglas, who turns ninety-five on December 9, 2011, blogs on MySpace. He writes about his political views (Douglas thinks he and other wealthy people should pay more taxes) spiced with personal issues such as how he faces daily life battling the after-effects of a 1996 stroke.

Born Issur Danielovitch, his parents were Russian Jewish immigrants who came to Amsterdam seeking a better life. The family was poor and lived in the last house on the left on Eagle Street in the East End. Locally, they were known as the Demsky family, and Kirk was called "Isadore" or "Izzy" Demsky. He had six sisters, most of whom ended up living in the Albany area.

His father, Herschel or Harry Demsky, was a ragman; Douglas said his father was "the toughest, strongest Jew in Amsterdam." His mother, Bryna, eventually separated from her strong-willed husband.

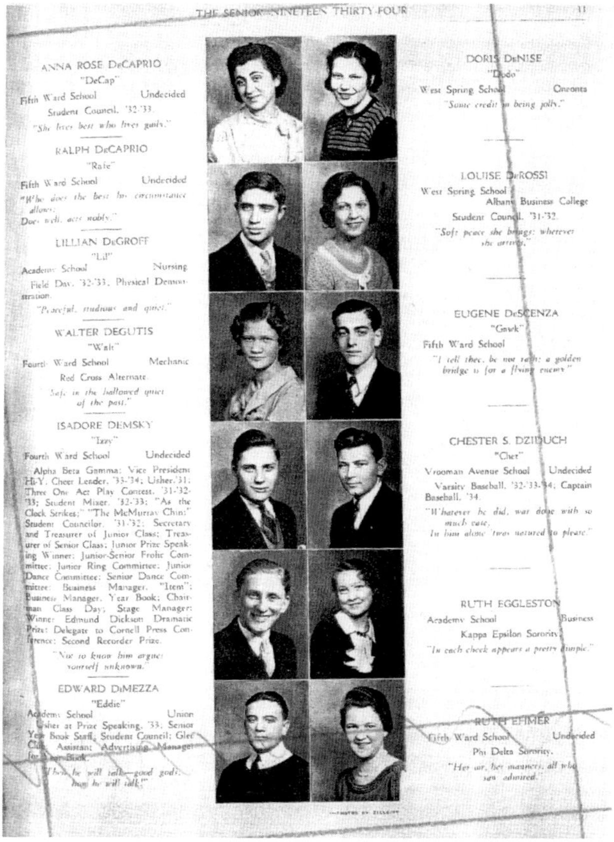

THE SENIOR NINETEEN THIRTY-FOUR 11

ANNA ROSE DeCAPRIO
"DeCap"
Fifth Ward School — Undecided
Student Council, '32-'33.
"She lives best who lives gaily."

RALPH DeCAPRIO
"Rafe"
Fifth Ward School — Undecided
"Who does the best his circumstance allows;
Does well, acts nobly."

LILLIAN DeGROFF
"Lil"
Academy School — Nursing
Field Day, '32-'33; Physical Demonstration.
"Peaceful, studious and quiet."

WALTER DEGUTIS
"Walt"
Fourth Ward School — Mechanic
Red Cross Alternate.
Safe in the hallowed quiet of the past."

ISADORE DEMSKY
"Izzy"
Fourth Ward School — Undecided
Alpha Beta Gamma; Vice President Hi-Y; Cheer Leader, '33-'34; Usher, '31; Three One Act Play Contest, '31-'32-'33; Student Mixer, '32-'33; "As the Clock Strikes;" "The McMurray Chin;" Student Councilor, '31-'32; Secretary and Treasurer of Junior Class; Treasurer of Senior Class; Junior Prize Speaking Winner; Junior-Senior Frolic Committee; Junior Ring Committee; Junior Dance Committee; Senior Dance Committee; Business Manager, "Item"; Business Manager, Year Book; Chairman Class Day; Stage Manager; Winner Edmund Dickson Dramatic Prize; Delegate to Cornell Press Conference; Second Recorder Prize.
"Not to know him argues yourself unknown."

EDWARD DiMEZZA
"Eddie"
Academy School — Union
Usher at Prize Speaking, '33; Senior Year Book Staff; Student Council; Glee Club; Assistant Advertising Manager for Year Book.
"Then he will talk—good gods! how he will talk!"

DORIS DeNISE
"Dodo"
West Spring School — Oneonta
"Some credit in being jolly."

LOUISE DeROSSI
West Spring School — Albany Business College
Student Council, '31-'32.
"Soft peace she brings; wherever she arrives."

EUGENE DeSCENZA
"Gawk"
Fifth Ward School
"I tell thee, be not rash; a golden bridge is for a flying enemy."

CHESTER S. DZIDUCH
"Chet"
Vrooman Avenue School — Undecided
Varsity Baseball, '32-'33-'34; Captain Baseball, '34.
"Whatever he did, was done with so much ease,
In him alone 'twas natured to please."

RUTH EGGLESTON
Academy School — Business
Kappa Epsilon Sorority.
"In each cheek appears a pretty dimple."

RUTH EFIMER
Fifth Ward School — Undecided
Phi Delta Sorority.
"Her air, her manners, all who saw admired."

Isadore Demsky's yearbook picture from Amsterdam. He became the actor Kirk Douglas. *Bob Cudmore.*

My grandfather Harry Cudmore, also an Eagle Street resident, said the bar crowd once had to leave O'Shaughnessy's Tavern on East Main at Eagle because "somebody said something about the Jews, and Harry Demsky is cleaning out the place."

Izzy Demsky was a standout in speech at Amsterdam High School and was mentored by English teacher Louise Livingston. He was a regular doughnut customer at Vidulich's Bakery on Guy Park Avenue. A high school cheerleader, he worked in men's clothes at Lurie's Department Store.

A childhood friend, Peter Riccio, convinced Demsky to try college, and both went off to St. Lawrence University, where Demsky starred on the wrestling team. He also started acting. He worked summers as a counselor at YMCA Camp Agaming in the Adirondacks while performing in plays at the nearby Tamarack Playhouse. It was at Tamarack that he changed his name to Kirk Douglas, keeping the "D" sound of Danielovitch and Demsky for his stage name.

Douglas went to New York City to study acting and served in the U.S. Navy in World War II. He was working after the war in New York theaters when a fellow actor, Lauren Bacall, convinced a movie producer to give Douglas a shot in Hollywood.

His first big hit was the movie *Champion*, in which Douglas played a conflicted boxer. He was nominated for an Academy Award. *Champion* was the initial offering when the former Tryon Theater opened on Main Street in downtown Amsterdam in 1949. The next year, Douglas came home and paid a visit to both Theodore Roosevelt Junior High and Wilbur H. Lynch High School.

Numerous movie roles followed, and in 1959, Douglas produced and starred in *Spartacus*. Douglas named his production company Bryna Productions to honor his mother. Douglas earned a place in movie history by breaking the blacklist of left-leaning Hollywood figures by listing Dalton Trumbo's screenplay contributions in the *Spartacus* credits.

In 1985, Douglas returned to Amsterdam for Kirk Douglas Day. A park in his honor was dedicated on Guy Park Avenue Extension by then governor Mario Cuomo. A parade was held on Guy Park Avenue.

Douglas then had a reunion with Wilfred "Wolfie" Churchitt, an Amsterdam man who had saved the actor from drowning when both were children. Douglas also visited with Sonya Jacobsen Seigal and her family. Seigal was a diligent chronicler of Douglas's movie career. Douglas installed a plaque in her memory at the Amsterdam Free Library.

During that visit home, Douglas spoke of his immigrant roots, saying his native Eagle Street was like a United Nations of nationalities with its Crocettis, Naples, Allens, Cudmores and Demskys.

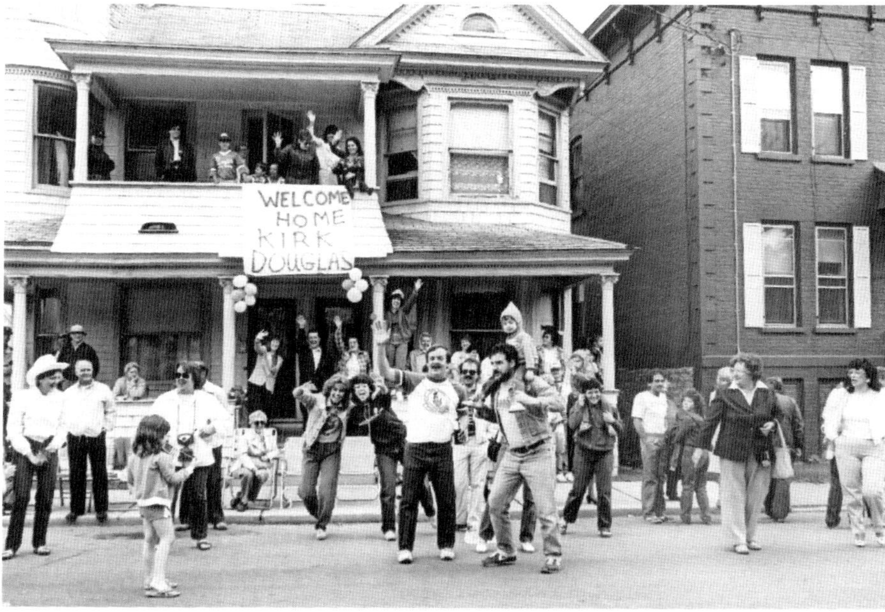

Tim and Gerri Zepperi welcome Amsterdam's Kirk Douglas Day Parade on Guy Park Avenue in 1985. *Walter Elwood Museum.*

He said, "My mother, God rest her soul, used to sit on that porch sometimes and say to me, 'Ah, America, such a wonderful land.'"

Douglas's autobiography, *The Ragman's Son*, was not popular in some quarters in Amsterdam because local people and the community were not always portrayed in a positive light.

Douglas spoke about anti-Semitism when he was a boy: "After school each day, I'd have to walk about twelve blocks to Hebrew school. I had to run the gauntlet, because every other street had a gang and they would always be waiting to catch the Jew boy."

Fooling the Ragman

Douglas wrote that his father left their Eagle Street home every day with his horse-drawn wagon, traveling the streets of Amsterdam yelling, "Rags, any rags!" The rags and scrap metal collected were sold to what we would call a recycling company.

Douglas wrote, "I'd help my father stuff the rags into burlap bags. I'd jab four holes in the top of the bag, lace a woman's discarded stocking through the holes, knot it, and add it to the pile of bags. I got to be quite good at stuffing ragbags, I don't think I'd have any trouble doing it today."

Amsterdam native Albert Roz said his late sister Clara used to scam Demsky when the ragman visited their grandfather, Albert Dzikowicz, on Crane Street at the top of Vrooman Avenue hill in the 1920s.

Demsky would leave his horse and wagon and sit with Dzikowicz in his cool grape arbor, playing cards and checkers and enjoying home-brewed alcohol.

Douglas wrote that his father always managed to find alcohol, even during Prohibition. Once, he got in trouble for drinking the ceremonial wine stored at his synagogue.

Roz said that while his grandfather and Demsky were out of sight in the grape arbor, his sister and her friends would "carefully remove a bag of rags from old man Demsky's buggy and drag it about one hundred feet to the corner of Crane and Church Street."

The girls patiently would wait for Demsky to resume his rag collection run with his horse and wagon and then sell him his own bag of rags, usually for twenty cents.

Roz wrote, "Wow, back in 1925, twenty cents would buy a lot of Mary Jane and other penny candy at Mruczek's candy store on Crane Street. Occasionally, young Isadore would join his father on these trips and Clara, her friends and Isadore would play and the girls could not sell rags to the ragman that day."

SINGER ARLENE FONTANA

Arlene Fontana worked hard to achieve success in a show business career that spanned close to forty years. The Amsterdam native performed on Broadway and appeared almost two thousand times in the national company of *Flower Drum Song*. She sang on TV programs, including *The Ed Sullivan Show*, and played nightclubs in New York, Chicago, London and Miami.

"Her greatest appeal was her energy and her appearance on stage," said Fontana's husband, theatrical agent Carmen LaVia. LaVia said that his late wife was a "powerful singer" who was always "so well prepared."

Born in 1936, Arlene was the only child of Marty and Palmera Masson Fontana. Marty Fontana came to Amsterdam as a young child from Genoa, Italy. A salesman for WCSS radio and other companies, Marty Fontana played trombone and violin in his own band, the Knights of Rhythm.

Arlene began taking tap, toe and ballet lessons at age ten. She studied piano. When she was fourteen, she did song-and-dance numbers in variety shows directed by local drama coach and later high school principal Bert DeRose.

In 1949, she attracted a regional following by appearing on the pioneer WRGB television program *Teenage Barn*. At the time, television was a rapidly growing medium, and there were several local music shows. Fontana sang with WRGB performers Gary Stevens and Earle Pudney; toured New York, Massachusetts and Vermont with *Teenage Barn*; and did summer stock at the Malden Bridge Playhouse.

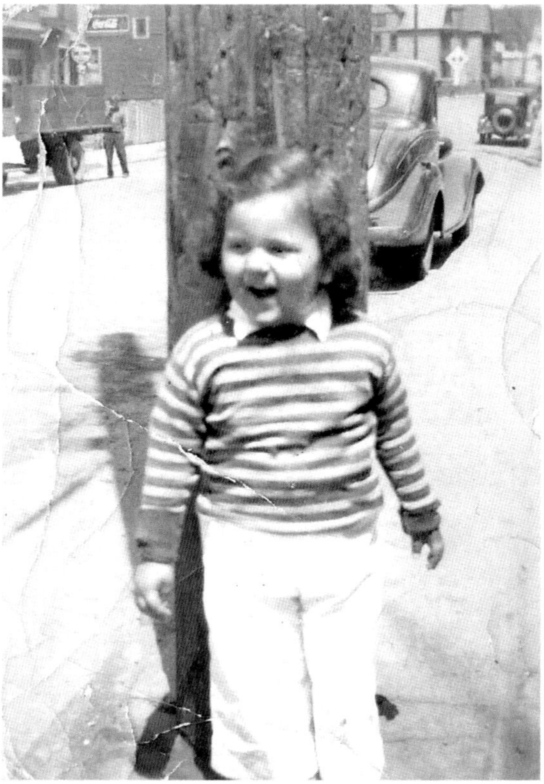

Arlene Fontana as a little girl in Amsterdam. *Carmen LaVia.*

In high school, she won an essay contest on the dangers of Communism and worked on a WCSS radio theater series directed by speech teacher Grace Rutherford.

When Fontana graduated from Wilbur H. Lynch High School in 1954, former Amsterdamian and family friend Joe Miller offered her a contract to sing at Miller's Shell Room Lounge in Miami. Fontana and her parents moved to Miami.

For a year, she sang in Miami nightclubs and then secured bookings in Pittsburgh, Washington, Detroit, Cleveland, Dallas, Houston and Las Vegas. She was a favorite on Television Nacional in pre-Castro Cuba. Her recording of "Easy" backed with "I'm in Love" on a forty-five record in the late 1950s did well in England, getting her club dates in London. Fontana was a friend of Bobby Darin then, and Darin recorded "Splish Splash" at the same time Fontana's record came out. She would tell friends in a humorous, self-deprecating way that Darin got "Splish Splash" a major hit, and she got "Easy."

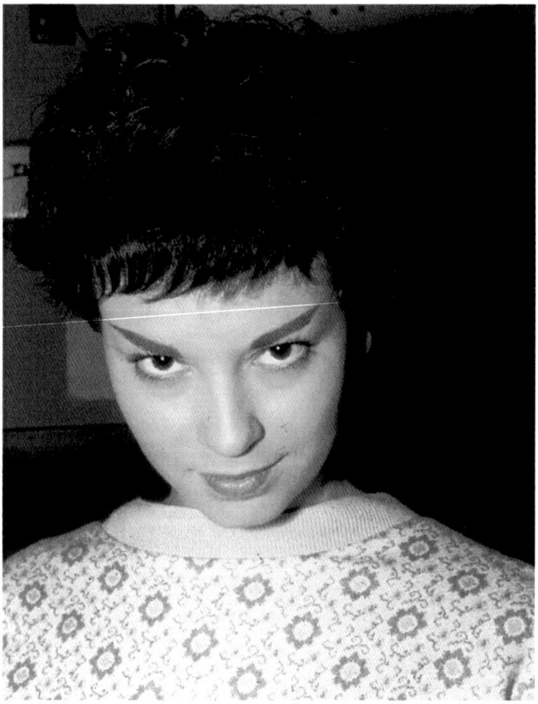

Arlene Fontana's publicity still for her first recording for Paris Records at age eighteen. *Carmen LaVia.*

Fontana appeared in the Broadway productions of *No, No Nanette* and *The Ritz*, and in the early '60s Richard Rodgers auditioned her for the role of Linda Low in the national touring company of *Flower Drum Song*. She played that role with its signature song, "I Enjoy Being a Girl," a record 1,972 times.

Over one thousand of those shows were done at the Thunderbird in Las Vegas, where Fontana met her future husband. She and Carmen LaVia married at St. Michael's Church in Amsterdam in 1965. The couple lived on the Upper East Side of Manhattan, where LaVia still works as an actors' and writers' agent for the Fifi Oscard Agency. He became Fontana's agent in 1972, and she continued to perform.

On television, she appeared on *The Ed Sullivan Show*, *The Merv Griffin Show*, *The Tonight Show* and *The Mike Douglas Show*. She acted in the soap operas *Another World* and *Loving*.

Other regional musical theater roles included the lead in *Irma La Douce*, Nellie Forbush in *South Pacific* and parts in *Pal Joey*, *Sweet Charity* and *Chicago*. She starred in the dramatic production of *Heaven Can Wait*. Among her nightclub credits were performances at the Drake in Chicago and *LaMaisonette* at the St. Regis Sheraton in New York City.

As a birthday present for her father, Fontana played a concert in 1971 at the then Coliseum Theatre in Latham, New York. Marty Fontana died in 1974.

In 1984, Arlene Fontana was diagnosed with breast cancer. By 1987, she was well enough to perform again on a cruise ship and other locations and was in her last stage show—*This Joint Is Jumpin'*— in 1988. Cancer returned, and she died of a stroke at New York's Memorial Sloan Kettering Hospital in May 1990. Her mother, Palmera, survived her daughter by more than a decade.

Arlene Fontana had a "sophisticated act," LaVia said, with "international songs translated from Italian and French." Her costumes were grand. Over the years, her musical directors included Jonathan Tunick, who also worked with Stephen Sondheim and John Devane, who went on to be music director of the Houston Symphony.

The Daiquiris

Salvatore J. Perillo has retired as general counsel to Mohawk Industries in Calhoun, Georgia, a firm descended from one of Amsterdam's carpet mills. He now heads a consulting firm. But when Perillo was a high school senior in 1963, his nickname was "Sam the Sham," and he played saxophone with the Daiquiris, an Amsterdam-based rock band.

Perillo's nickname came from a group called Sam the Sham and the Pharaohs, who produced one blockbuster hit: "Woolly Bully." The Daiquiris, however, were not one-hit wonders.

Playing covers of James Brown songs and other soul and rock music, the "Dacs" (as they were known) played at night spots such as Russo's in Amsterdam and the Glove Inn in Gloversville. Jake and Jenny Ketchum recruited them for the Glove Inn on Steele Avenue Extension, where cars would line up for a mile when the sign went up saying, "The Dacs Are Back."

The band spent the summer of 1965 at the Glen Lake Casino near Lake George and played clubs in Albany. They were popular at fraternity parties at Union, Rensselaer, Syracuse and even Penn State.

Getting Together

First organized as the Valiant Four in the early 1960s, the band featured Perillo, bandleader Norb Sherbunt on guitar, Bob Olbrycht on drums and guitarist Bob Dietrich, all from Amsterdam.

Dietrich left to go into military service, and Ed Emmrich joined the band, now renamed the Daiquiris. Bill Vrooman made the Dacs a five-piece group in 1964, adding his skills as a horn and keyboard player.

Sherbunt "really put the band together, he had the ideas," said Perillo. Sherbunt was a 1960 Amsterdam High School graduate and a

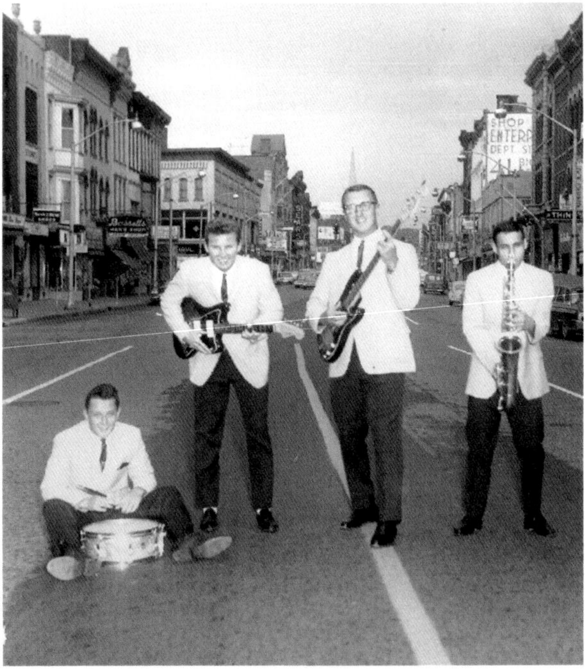

The Daiquiris—a rock band made up of Bob Olbrycht, Ed Dietrich, Norb Sherbunt and Sal Perillo—pose on Amsterdam's East Main Street in 1963. *Norb Sherbunt.*

student at Syracuse University when the band began. Today, he is an Amsterdam attorney.

The Daiquiris broke up in the late 1960s, mainly because Sherbunt was having difficulty balancing the demands of the band and his studies at Albany Law School.

Two of Sherbunt's ideas were a dress code and publicity pictures. Band members visited proprietor Paul Gutenberg at Mortan's men's store in 1963 and bought dark pants and light blue sport coats. Wearing this sharp attire, the band went to Paul Masto's photography studio on East Main Street.

After the standard studio pose, Masto suggested another shot. Album covers of the day showed bands on ladders and looking out windows. Masto stopped traffic on East Main Street and took a picture of the band in the middle of what was then a busy thoroughfare.

The members of the Daiquiris are alive and well today, but the same can't be said for many of the buildings and almost all the businesses in that 1963 photo.

The buildings in the foreground still exist, but the structures in the background were demolished for the downtown mall. A Walt Disney movie was playing at the Tryon Theater. Other vanished downtown landmarks include the Enterprise Store, Holzheimer and Shaul, Bassett's men's shop, Sears, Things Shoes, the Mohawk Theater, Kresge's and the Amsterdam Hotel.

The Daiquiris have pursued other careers, but all maintain an interest in music. In fact, Norb Sherbunt did the sound and lights for his son's alternative band, Tunnel.

Perillo went to work in the finance department of what was then Mohasco Industries in Amsterdam in 1970. Carpet production had already moved south, and when the company moved corporate offices to Georgia in the 1980s, Perillo followed. He went to law school while on the job and became general counsel. He has played with bands in Georgia.

After the Daiquiris broke up, Ed Emmrich played in wedding and banquet bands while working at Schenectady General Electric, including a stint as manager of the employee store. He lives in Amsterdam and is retired.

Bob "Bubba Boy" Olbrycht was the youngest member of the Daiquiris, recruited to play at a Senior Day event in 1963, when he was a high school sophomore. His previous experience was as a drummer in Polish polka bands, but he learned to be a rock drummer. He continued playing in blues and rock bands while pursuing a career as a graphic artist. Today, Olbrycht owns Ricmar Design and Print on Edson Street in Amsterdam.

According to Perillo, Bill Vrooman, who joined the band after the 1963 picture, is a hospital administrator who lives in Florida.

Artist Mary Van der Veer

In the years before World War I, Mary Van der Veer smoked cigarettes, bobbed her blond hair and traveled on crutches and in wheelchairs between Holland and Paris, where she studied with artist James Whistler.

Born on a farm near Fort Hunter in 1865, Mary painted numerous oils, pastels and watercolors in her remarkable life. Many of these paintings are prized possessions in private collections in the Mohawk Valley and elsewhere. She primarily painted flowers, portraits and landscapes.

The daughter of John and Jennue Van der Veer, Mary was stricken with polio at age three. Her legs were paralyzed, and her hands and back were deformed. The family moved to Crane's Hollow Road in the town of Amsterdam, where an accident threatened Mary's sight when she was eight.

The late historian Katherine Strobeck wrote in her book *Mohawk Valley Happenings*, "Mary's father was painting a wall with a type of whitewash known as muresco. Mary tipped the solution down on her head into her

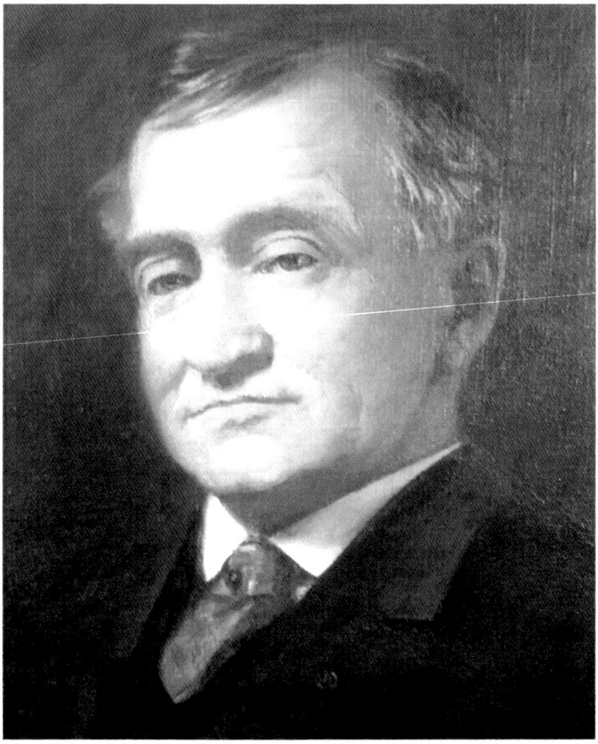

Portrait of an *Unknown Gentleman* by Mary Van der Veer. *Tom Foster.*

eyes. A family member rushed to the milk house and threw a pan of milk into Mary's eyes, saving her sight."

Their daughter's artistic talent was valued by the Van der Veer family, and they had the means to provide her with a proper education. Mary attended the National Academy of Design in New York City, and her pictures were displayed at the Chicago World's Fair and the Paris Exhibition. She left for Paris and studied with Whistler. Her self-portrait was chosen for a show Whistler held for his students in 1900. She also spent time back in Amsterdam and elsewhere in America, for example holding a one-woman show in Philadelphia.

Mary's father was a contractor who built houses on Amsterdam's Market Hill. He converted a barn on Arnold Avenue into a house and studio for Mary, using the services of architect P.P. Cassidy. The dwelling was the subject of a *House Beautiful* article in 1915 entitled "How 'Barneo' Became 'Little House.'"

"At the back of 'little house,' on either side of her door, Mary had a small garden plot of her own—cultivated flowers on one side and wild flowers on the other," wrote Helen Ireland Hays of Johnstown in a monograph about the artist. Hays said that young people found Mary "sympathetic and helpful."

After World War I, Mary lived for a time in Veere, Holland, where her ancestors had resided. After moving back to Arnold Avenue in Amsterdam, Mary painted flowers, portraits and Sacandaga Reservoir scenes.

She went to Philadelphia to do a portrait but fell and hurt her back. "She was never again able to do large pieces," Strobeck said. A later back injury hurt her hands, and she stopped painting.

In 1932, eighty-five of her paintings were displayed at the home of Elliott Boice on Guy Park Avenue in Amsterdam in a benefit for the YMCA. That home became the Boice Funeral Home. A newspaper review in the *Recorder* stated, "The pastels, which Miss Van der Veer handles as well as any contemporary artist, were the source of special interest to many."

Mary Van der Veer died in 1945 at the age of seventy-nine. Many attended a Daughters of the American Revolution memorial program organized by local art teacher Marion Rulison in Van der Veer's honor. In a 1964 essay, her niece Marie L. Gilbert wrote, "In a competitive masculine field, not noted in the past for its financial remunerations, Miss V. was able to support herself and to travel." Gilbert, who posed for a Van der Veer portrait as a young, "wiggling" child, added that her aunt's blue eyes twinkled, and she had "a tongue sometimes peppery and a merry laugh."

Several of the artist's paintings are in the collection of the Walter Elwood Museum in Amsterdam. Old Fort Johnson Historic Site mounted an exhibition of her work in 2007.

Stolen Painting?

One of the most prized possessions of Amsterdam's Century Club was a Van der Veer painting of one of the founders of the women's club. The painting, donated in 1933, disappeared some years later and may have been stolen.

The portrait was of M. Annie Allen Trapnell, an Amsterdam native born in 1836, who taught school in several upstate cities. The scholarly rector of St. Ann's Church in Amsterdam, Reverend W.H. Trapnell, courted Annie for many years. They married in 1872, when she was thirty-five and he was sixty. They moved to Maryland, where the reverend died four months later.

Returning to Amsterdam, Annie Trapnell spent the remaining thirty-six years of her life promoting community activities, including the library and orphans' home.

Trapnell was the driving force in establishing the Century Club in 1895. The twenty-five charter members each invited three women to join, at first limiting the club to one hundred, hence its name. When Trapnell died in 1908, the club sent 250 white roses to her funeral, one for each member of the growing club. The current clubhouse at 130 Guy Park Avenue was built in 1934.

THE CAMACHO FAMILY

Aldelmo Camacho spent his early years on a farm near Yauco, a small city on the south side of the island of Puerto Rico. The youngest of ten children, Camacho joined the army in 1942 and served as a medical surgery technician. After the war, he attended Business College, where he met his future wife, Ernestina Perez. In 1948, they were married, and the family grew with the birth of two daughters.

Jobs were scarce in Puerto Rico. Two of Aldelmo's brothers had moved to America and settled in Amsterdam, attracted by newspaper ads from the carpet industry. In 1950, Aldelmo left his family and arrived in Amsterdam on a Sunday in June. He had his first job the next day, making pocketbooks for Central Leather.

"When I came here, you could have a job, quit the job and get another job in that same building with another company," Aldelmo said. "If you didn't have a job here it was because you didn't want to work."

Aldelmo stayed in Amsterdam for four months but returned to Yauco because he missed his family. There was still no work in Puerto Rico, so Aldelmo headed north again. This time, he ran a milling machine at Collette's Manufacturing, preparing rubber for tennis and beach balls.

Within a few months, Tina and the children moved to Amsterdam, and Tina began work at Amsterdam Glove. Their first home was in the former Amsterdam Hotel on Main Street. Apartments followed and then their own houses on Academy Street and, later, Bunn Street.

There were only a few Latinos in Amsterdam in the early 1950s. "When we came in it was just Puerto Ricans and Cubans," Aldelmo said. Today, Amsterdam's growing Latino population has roots in Columbia, Costa Rica, Mexico and other countries. After decades of decline, the Amsterdam city population was reported as 18,620 in the 2010 census, an increase of 265 compared to 2000. The percentage of Latinos in 2010 was reported as 26.2 percent.

In 1953, the Camachos were instrumental in forming the Spanish American Club, which closed in 2004. Its Milton Avenue clubhouse is now a church.

Aldelmo and Tina worked hard. Tina held jobs at Chalmer's Button Shop, Hanover Dress, Martin Jay Dress and Mohawk Dress. She also earned her high school diploma and attended Fulton-Montgomery Community College.

"We made an honest dollar every place we went," Tina said. "We started at seventy-five cents an hour and then it went up to a dollar an hour. We lived on that."

Aldelmo worked several years at the Naval Depot in Scotia and then was a dress cutter at Hanover's. Hanover's closed its Amsterdam plant in 1972 and wanted Aldelmo to relocate to Vermont. Instead, the Camachos returned to Puerto Rico.

"We went back, and I got a job in San Juan cutting dresses," Aldelmo said. "But I was in San Juan, and she was in Yauco, a hundred miles apart, and we stayed just seven weeks. When we left Puerto Rico, it was one way of living. When we went back, it was too different. It was a different country for us."

Back in Amsterdam, Aldelmo secured jobs at Coleco and then Gem Urethane, Bojud Knitting and General Electric before his retirement.

"This town came to be more important than the town where I was born," said Aldelmo, who has a reputation for his skill at dominoes. "This town for me is like my hometown. It's where I've raised my family and where my grandchildren are. Everything for me is here."

The Camachos have eight grandchildren and six great-grandchildren. They currently reside in Fort Hunter at the home of their daughter Ida Slansky, who is retired. Their other daughter is Lillian Murillo, who works for the New York State Energy Research and Development Agency.

Alex Torres

Latin bandleader Alex Torres has had a major impact on the cultural life of Amsterdam and the surrounding area. Alex's parents, like the Camachos, came from the southern part of Puerto Rico and moved to the South Bronx. When Alex was a teenager, the family relocated to Amsterdam. Alex had a hard time adjusting to small-town life—until he formed his band in 1980. Alex Torres and His Latin Orchestra have played for President Bill Clinton and at New York gubernatorial inaugurations and hundreds of venues throughout the Northeast.

Torres was one of the founders of Centro Civico, Amsterdam's Latino community organization, now housed in impressive quarters on East Main

Street. Director Ladan Alomar is hopeful that a longtime dream of an East End park can become a reality.

In a 1999 interview, when he still operated El Palacio Musicale, an Amsterdam music store, Torres outlined his objections to the phrase "melting pot."

"I prefer a salad bowl," he said. "And I mean everyone loves salad, right? And you have lettuce, tomatoes, cucumbers, yet they're all individual pieces, but they all go very well. And you can taste them all separately."

Asked to describe the Latino part of the salad, Torres smiled and replied, "Jalapenos, hot peppers, anything that's colorful and fragrant."

MARY—AN IMMIGRANT'S STORY

The descendants of a woman who came to Amsterdam in 1913 have lovingly preserved the story of how this remarkable individual kept her family of nine children together after her husband's unexpected death.

Mary Teresa Sieminowicz considered herself Polish but came to America from the then-Austrian village of Mariampol, an area now part of Russia. As the late Amsterdam pastor Reverend Walter Czechowicz has pointed out, there was no country of Poland during the great wave of Polish migration to America in the early twentieth century. But in their hearts, Czechowicz said, these immigrants to America were Polish.

Mary was seventeen when an agent came to Mariampol looking for "talented and self-sufficient people" willing to relocate to the United States. Mary's mother sold the family's baby pigs to finance the $100 cost of Mary's venture. A seamstress in the village told Mary about opportunities in Amsterdam, New York. The day after arriving at Ellis Island in June 1913, the young immigrant boarded a train for Amsterdam.

Local homeowners of the time met the trains and offered lodging to newcomers. Mary rented space on VanDerveer Street for three dollars a month and found work as a spinner at Morris Mills. She was paid six dollars each fifty-five-hour workweek.

Mary moved several times and met John Leszczynski, the brother of a woman she had boarded with at a residence on Jay Street. Mary and John were married on November 22, 1915, at St. John's Church on Park Hill, and they lived on Grand Street. Mary continued working at Morris Mills, and John worked at Broadalbin Knitting Mills. Mary sent $5 and $10 contributions periodically to her mother to pay off her $100 debt for passage

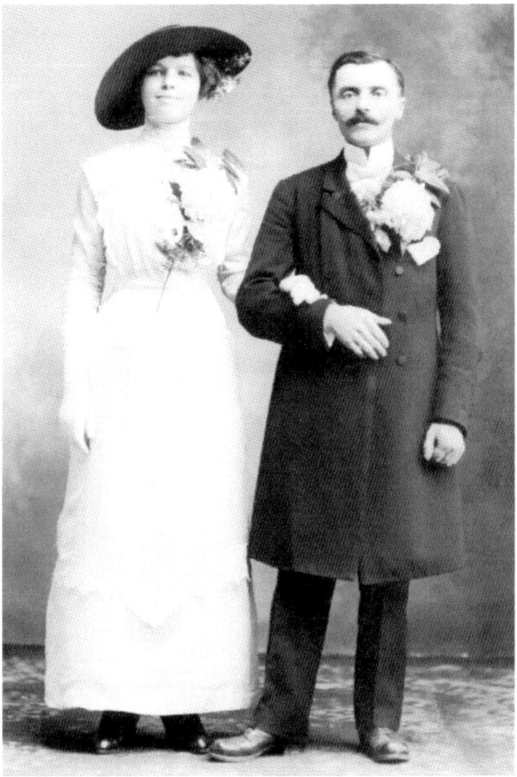

Immigrants Mary and John Leszczynski on their wedding day in Amsterdam, November 22, 1915. *Kathy Snyder.*

to America. Her mother died a few years after World War I, and Mary lost contact with her relatives overseas.

In all, Mary and John had eleven children, nine of whom survived to be adults. The family moved to Cohoes, where both parents worked in the mills.

Mary and John moved to a two-hundred-acre farm on Big Murray Road on the outskirts of Broadalbin in the town of Galway, Saratoga County, in 1919.

About 1929, the family moved back to Amsterdam, exchanging properties with a family on Swan Street. The next year, the Broadalbin farmhouse burned down, and the exchange family disappeared. Not able to afford both mortgages, Mary and John moved back to the farm, converting the chicken coop into living quarters. John continued working at Broadalbin Knitting Mill while the family began building a new farmhouse.

In May 1937, John died of a heart attack while working at the mill. Mary was a forty-year-old widow with two sons and seven daughters, ranging in age from three to eighteen. She was determined to finish their farmhouse.

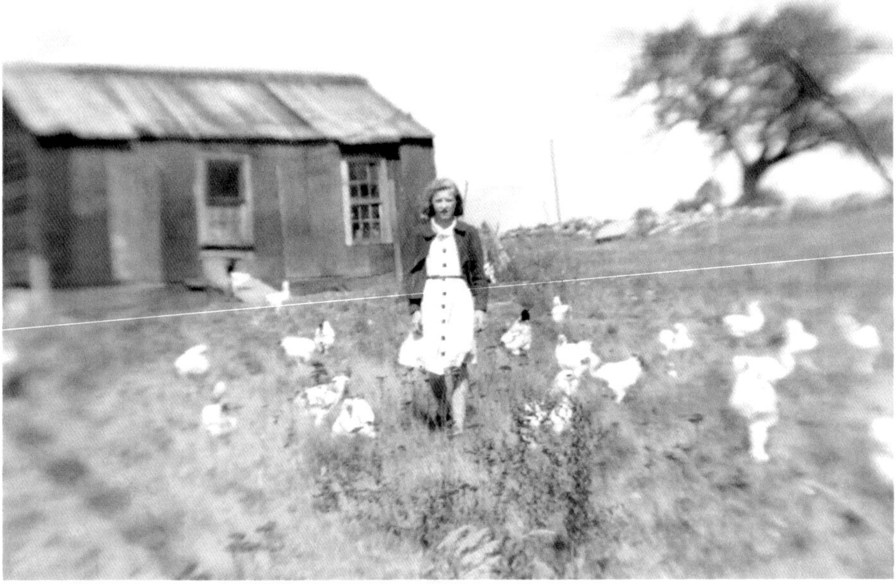

Mary's daughter Stella Leszczynski in front of the chicken coop on Mary's farm. *Kathy Snyder.*

Most livestock and farm equipment were sold. She continued her child rearing and farm work and tried to find jobs outside the home. The older children quit school and went to work to raise money. The family moved into the farmhouse that November.

"Both the will and the body of Mary Leszczynski are as strong as the concrete foundation of the new home in which she and her nine children live triumphantly," wrote the *Albany Knickerbocker News* in a feature story in 1938. The headline read, "Undaunted woman erects new home; carries on after death of husband to move her nine children from their quarters in chicken house."

In the 1940s, the older children secured jobs that brought in extra income. Her children married, and grandchildren were born. In 1947, Mary became an American citizen.

Mary died in 1983 at age eighty-six. Daughter Jennie continued to live on the farm until her death in 1999. Late that year, the family sold the farm.

"Her strong work ethic and determination serve as an inspiration to all of us who share in her heritage," wrote Mary's granddaughter Katherine Slezak Snyder of Amsterdam in a family book compiled in the year 2000.

Snyder said, "Over the years, Mary's dreams of great opportunity were replaced by language barriers, family loss and economic difficulty.

She became widowed with nine children, yet managed to keep her family together through the toughest of times."

Mary's Children

Two of Mary's children, Jennie and Steve, did not marry and lived on the farm throughout their lives. Jennie worked for several years at local knitting mills but also raised sheep and harvested crops on the farm. Steve raised dairy and beef cattle throughout his life.

Two children moved out of state. Marcella worked for several years as an engraver at General Electric. She married, had two children and relocated to North Carolina, where she helped manage her family's business: boarding horses. Henry became an electrician in the navy, married and had three children. After the navy, he worked for the Union Pacific Railroad and lived in Arkansas.

Helen had four children and worked in the capacitor department at General Electric. Lottie graduated from business school. She did secretarial work for several years, married, had four children, went to nursing school and worked as a nurse at a local hospital. Now retired, she does volunteer

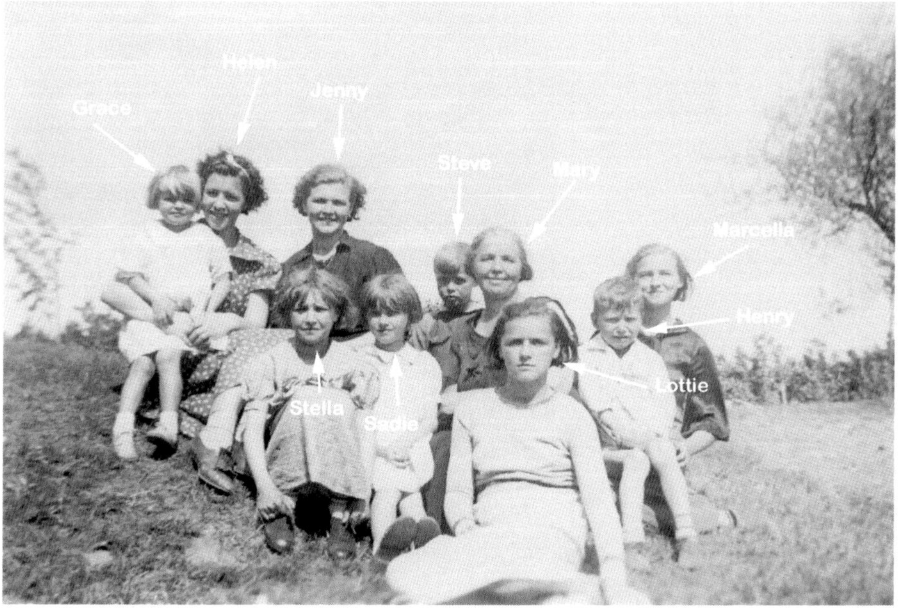

Mary Leszczynski and her children at Mary's farm. *Kathy Snyder.*

work with a soup kitchen and the Red Cross. Stella worked at General Electric, married, had three children, did waitressing and worked in retail for several years. She now volunteers at a local hospital. Sadie did secretarial work several years for General Electric, married and had two children. Then she did secretarial work at a doctor's office. Grace became a registered nurse. She was operating room supervisor at a local hospital and then did private-duty nursing. She married a physician, worked in his practice and had several stepchildren.

THREE MEMORABLE MAYORS OF AMSTERDAM

Mayor Akin

Growing up in the then solidly Democratic Fourth Ward of Amsterdam in the 1950s, I have memories of election days in which school-age bullies gave their usual targets a free pass and instead went on the prowl for suspected Republicans.

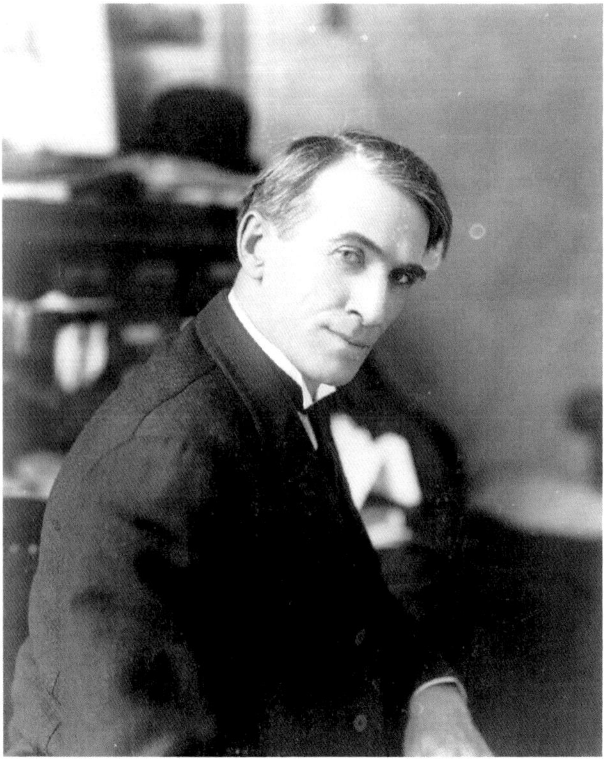

Theron Akin in 1911, during his one term in Congress. Akin went on to be Amsterdam's most controversial mayor. *Library of Congress.*

Historian Hugh Donlon has reported that political passions reached a peak in Amsterdam long before that—during the administration of Mayor Theron Akin.

Born in Johnstown in 1855, Akin went to school in Amsterdam and became a dentist and farmer. He lived in what is now Fort Johnson. His father, Ethan, was a farmer and landowner who lived in the Old Fort itself. In 1905, the Montgomery County Historical Society bought the fort from the Akin family for $5,900.

In 1909, Theron Akin led the campaign to incorporate the area around the Old Fort as the village of Akin and became its first president.

Akin was elected to Congress as a Progressive Republican in 1910, telling the *New York Times*, "I got close to the people and told them the truth." Akin used the campaign slogan "The Full Dinner Pail." His posters showed a dinner pail empty except for a lemon.

In 1911, the *Washington Post* described Akin as an insurgent Democrat, quoting Robert McKeever of Schenectady, who described an anti-speeding campaign started by Akin in the village that then bore his name.

"Dr. Akin is a sort of town marshal in his village," McKeever said.

> *He is the owner of an automobile, but he doesn't like scorching, and when the autoists went speeding too rapidly by his house he determined to stop 'em. He served notice that anyone caught going at a greater speed than 15 miles per hour through Akin would be dealt with summarily. The sign didn't have a bit of an effect.*
>
> *Then the doctor early one morning secured a stout rope and stretched it across the road. He waited for the scorchers, and the first one, of course had to stop. It was not long until there were a score of impatient automobilists lined up. All were fined, and if they were caught again they were imprisoned. This put an end to the scorching in Akin, New York.*

Former Amsterdam city attorney Bob Going wrote that while Akin was serving in Congress, his colleagues thought so little of him that they voted to rename the village of Akin as Fort Johnson, over his objections.

Akin was defeated in his congressional reelection bid in 1912 and failed again in a run for Congress in 1914. He then began a long campaign to be elected Amsterdam mayor, much to the chagrin of the city establishment.

The common council even got the state legislature to pass a charter change requiring a year's residency for mayoral candidates, but Governor Al Smith vetoed the measure.

Akin was elected Amsterdam mayor in 1919. He won endorsement of all parties in spirited primary contests that year.

Shortly after taking office, Akin suspended the police chief and appointed new members to the city health board. He began an investigation of gambling in Amsterdam. He disguised himself as a hoodlum and was arrested to probe conditions in the city jail.

In 1921, he defeated Leon Hall by 3,274 votes to win a second term as mayor, once again with the backing of both Democrats and Republicans. Two days after the election, Akin fired the city public works commissioner.

Going wrote, "From what I've read in the old Common Council minutes he didn't seem to get along with anybody. There were continuous efforts to have him removed from office."

In 1922, Akin married Jenny Bornt, the last of four wives, according to the family website. In 1923, he vetoed pay raises for police and firemen.

Donlon wrote of the Akin years, "It was a time of hatreds, barrages of unparalleled personal attacks, and with pamphleteering innuendos so gross and vicious that some of the campaign literature was later prized as collectors' items."

Republican Carl S. Salmon was elected mayor in 1923 and served for three terms of relative calm. Shortly after Salmon's election, Akin delivered a farewell address in the manner of George Washington. In 1925, the former mayor declined an offer from the Democrats to run for state senate. In 1927, he ran unsuccessfully for mayor once again.

According to the family website, when Akin died in 1933, he was "friendless and penniless." He was buried at Pine Grove Cemetery in Tribes Hill.

Mayor Carter

From time to time in the 1930s, Amsterdam mayor Arthur Carter would get in a police car for a trip to Washington, D.C., to visit his friend, President Franklin D. Roosevelt.

Lionel Fallows, son of Carter's sister Nellie, said Roosevelt came through for the Amsterdam mayor. It was a triumvirate, Fallows said, with three Democrats in power—Carter, New York governor Herbert Lehman and Roosevelt. There was money for the golf course, named for Carter, and money for other Amsterdam projects. Fallows said Carter could have done more, but political opponents sometimes stymied the mayor.

Arthur Carter was born in 1897 in Kidderminster, England, a center of the English carpet trade that was a source of carpet-savvy immigrants who helped build Amsterdam's leading industry. The youngest of several

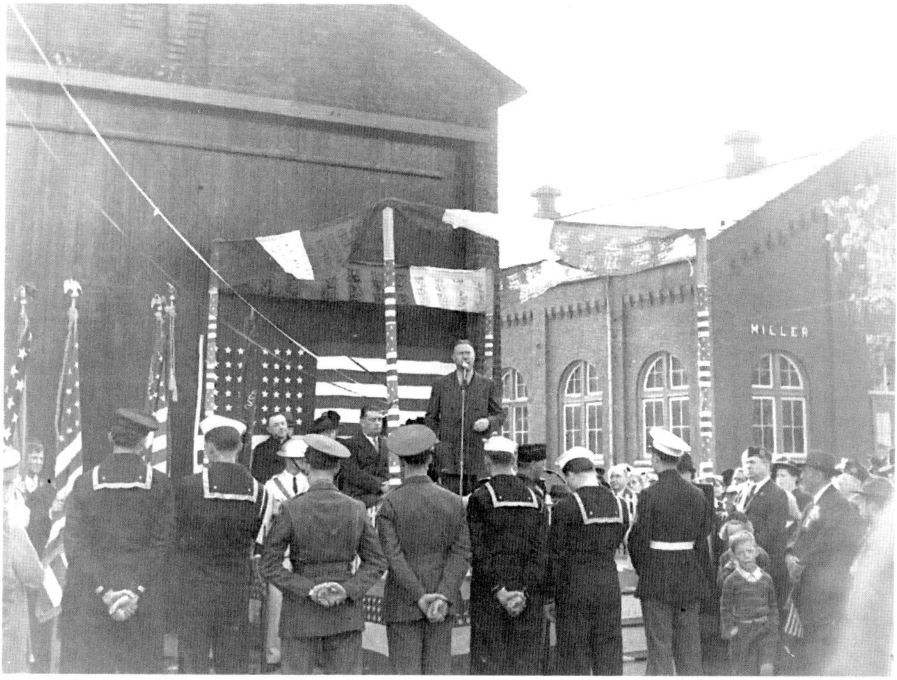

Mayor Arthur Carter addressing an Amsterdam crowd. *John Maney photo from the Montgomery County Department of History and Archives.*

children, he came to America when he was nine and lived with his family on Lefferts Street in the East End.

Carter served in the U.S. Army in World War I. He never took to carpet making, working instead in the wholesale grocery business. In 1923, he married Lorraine Conrad. They did not have children.

Fallows said he did not know if his favorite uncle went beyond the eighth grade but said Carter took correspondence courses.

The year after his marriage, Carter started working for the State Comptroller's Office in Albany as an auditor and got to know Roosevelt.

Carter ran unsuccessfully for office in Amsterdam three times. Fallows said his uncle was terrified at first by public speaking but through practice became an expert at holding an audience.

In 1933, Carter was elected mayor—a year after Roosevelt was elected president. Carter always enjoyed strong support among Amsterdam's Polish immigrants in the Fourth Ward and counted Reid Hill businessman Michael Wytrwal as one of his strongest supporters. Carter was reelected five times, the last time in 1941. He was also Montgomery County Democratic Party chairman.

In 1943, Carter left the mayor's job for the military. A temporary mayor, John Klubakowski, served until Wilbur H. Lynch, who had been school superintendent, was elected mayor in 1944.

Awarded the rank of major, Carter served as military mayor of Bologna, Italy, during the Allied occupation. He learned Italian on the job.

When he returned to America, Carter went into broadcasting. He did a program on WSNY radio in Schenectady called *Carter's Comments*. In 1948, Carter was the principal founder of Community Service Broadcasting Corporation and radio station WCSS in Amsterdam. Carter was station president until 1953. He later worked in the financial field.

In 1963, Carter was prevailed upon by the Democratic Party to oppose Republican Marcus Breier in a race for mayor. Breier won.

Arthur Carter died on August 29, 1983, at age eighty-six. He and his wife lived at 4 Beacon Avenue on Market Hill. He was a vestryman at St. Ann's Episcopal Church, a Mason, an Elk and past commander of the James T. Bergen American Legion Post. He is buried in St. Mary's Cemetery, as his wife was Roman Catholic.

Mayor Breier

Marcus I. Breier, a Republican, had never run for elected office when he handily defeated Carter in the mayoral election of 1963.

While serving as mayor, Breier continued to operate his clothing outerwear company, Breier's of Amsterdam. Breier would work at city hall in the morning and go to his clothing factory on Edson Street in the afternoon.

Breier was born in Brooklyn and went to Cornell University and Cornell Law School. He practiced law for a year before joining the family men's sports clothes business, named Marcus Breier & Son's in honor of his grandfather.

The business had been based in New York City but was lured upstate during the Depression. Benjamin Breier, Marcus's father, established a manufacturing plant on Leonard Street in Amsterdam while the firm's showroom was at the Empire State Building in Manhattan.

"Nothing was easy," Marcus Breier recalled. "My father worked in Amsterdam all week and came home to New York City on the weekends. It's impossible to know the sacrifices people made in the Depression."

Benjamin Breier is credited in a 1940s Amsterdam Chamber of Commerce publication with being among the first to introduce lightweight wind- and weather-resistant jackets in America. The Breier brand name for these garments was Bantamac. Bantamac jackets were used by the army and navy in World War II.

Ultimately, the future mayor took charge of the family business. Still later, the firm was sold, and Breier started Breier's of Amsterdam, also an outerwear maker.

Breier credited state Supreme Court justice Felix J. Aulisi, a longtime friend, with encouraging him to enter politics. "He put the bug in my ear," Breier said.

During Breier's term, from 1964 through 1967, urban renewal began, the public safety building on Guy Park Avenue extension was started and Veterans Park on Locust Avenue was developed. Breier also convinced the then New York Central Railroad not to abandon Amsterdam when urban renewal claimed the former downtown station. The new station was built in the West End, but still in the city.

Amsterdam voters had approved a charter change in the late 1950s stipulating that a mayor could serve only one four-year term. Breier, therefore, was prevented by law from seeking a second term.

Longtime public works official John P. Gomulka was elected mayor in 1967. While Gomulka was in office, the city charter was changed again, and Gomulka served three four-year terms, ending in 1979. Mario Villa was then elected mayor and served two consecutive four-year terms starting in 1980 and a separate four-year term beginning in 1992. Gomulka and Villa thus served longer than any other city mayor so far, although Mayor Carter won more elections, since he was running every two years.

After 1967, Breier went on to serve multiple terms on the Montgomery County Board of Supervisors, including a stint as chairman. Breier wrote a history of Amsterdam, available at the local library. He was a member of the Montgomery County Bar Association and of Congregation Sons of Israel in Amsterdam, where he served as its president on multiple occasions. In later years, Breier and his wife, Eleanore Cramer Breier, spent half the year in Doral, Florida, and half the year at their home on McClellan Avenue in Amsterdam. Marcus Breier died at age ninety-seven on May 15, 2010. He is buried at Temple of Israel Cemetery in Cranesville.

It was during Breier's term as mayor that I held a summer job in city government, working as a laborer for the Department of Public Works in 1964. It was the only time in my life that I worked hard for a living.

MICHAEL WYTRWAL—THE POLISH MAYOR OF AMSTERDAM

Long before Polish-American John Gomulka was elected mayor of Amsterdam in 1967, Michael J. Wytrwal, who never held elected office, was for all intents and purposes the Polish mayor of the Carpet City.

Wytrwal was born near Krakow, Poland, in 1882 and immigrated to Scranton, Pennsylvania, when he was fourteen with his mother, Sophie, who then returned to their native land to retrieve another son. Sophie and her other son died in Poland. Wytrwal worked in Scranton's coal mines for six months and then moved to Reid Hill, one of Amsterdam's Polish enclaves. There, he started a candy and ice cream business.

He married Mamie Brudzdowski in 1904 and sold life insurance. Mamie died two years later in childbirth. In 1907, Wytrwal married Mamie's sister, Josephine. He fathered seven children, the son from his first marriage plus five daughters and another son from his second marriage. The Wytrwals took up residence in the Brudzdowskis' two-family home at 26 Cornell Street.

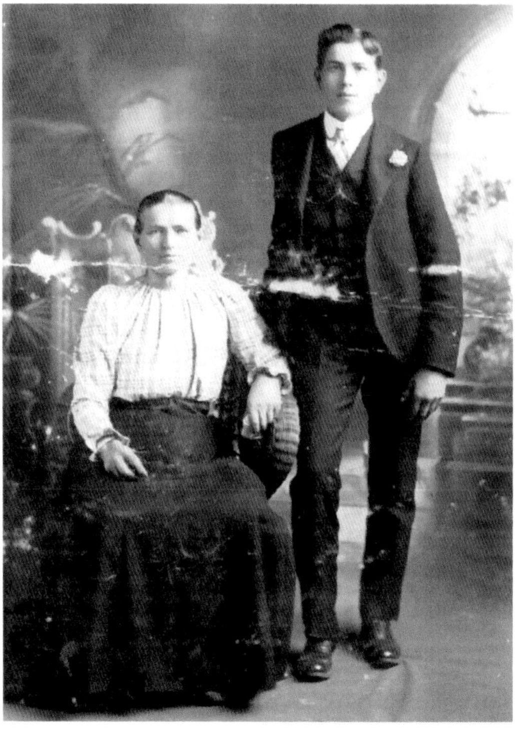

Sophie Wytrwal and her son Michael in 1895. *Stanley Zurawel.*

In 1911, he was a founder of Amsterdam's Polish National Alliance (PNA), today located at Reid and Church Streets. The PNA is a social organization that also provides life insurance to Polish Americans.

Wytrwal became an entrepreneur. He founded a pharmacy in 1910, later operated by a daughter and son-in-law as Krupczak's Pharmacy on Hibbard Street. Next door was Wytrwal's Furniture, managed by one of Wytrwal's sons. M.J. Wytrwal Coal and Oil, started in 1926, was on James Street. Wytrwal was a founder of what was known as the Polish bank, Amsterdam Federal Savings and Loan on Reid Street. He built homes in Amsterdam and was part owner of a Fort Plain knitting mill.

The local Polish people constantly approached Wytrwal for assistance getting work, even for help with marital and other personal problems. During the Depression, Polish people were often too proud to beg. Wytrwal let it be known that he enjoyed "welfare peanut butter" handed out to the needy. He bought jars of the peanut butter from destitute friends.

In the 1933 election, Wytrwal helped English native Arthur Carter win the mayor's race as a Democrat. Carter served twelve years with Wytrwal's support in the predominately Polish Fourth Ward. President Franklin Roosevelt named Wytrwal to head National Recovery Act programs in Montgomery County.

One grandchild said Wytrwal was eloquent in both Polish and English and was a broker between the Polish-speaking community and the English-speaking power structure. The grandchildren remember Christmas Eves when the needy always found a seat at the family table. Wytrwal doted on his fifteen grandchildren, one of whom drove him places when his failing eyesight made it impossible for him to drive himself.

He was a role model for granddaughter Mary Anne Krupsak, whose parents operated the family's pharmacy. Krupsak ate lunch at her grandparents' home every day when she attended St. Stanislaus School nearby. Krupsak saw a constant parade of people seeking assistance from her grandfather.

Wytrwal's wife, Josephine, died in 1956. Michael Wytrwal lived to see Krupsak elected to the state assembly in 1968.

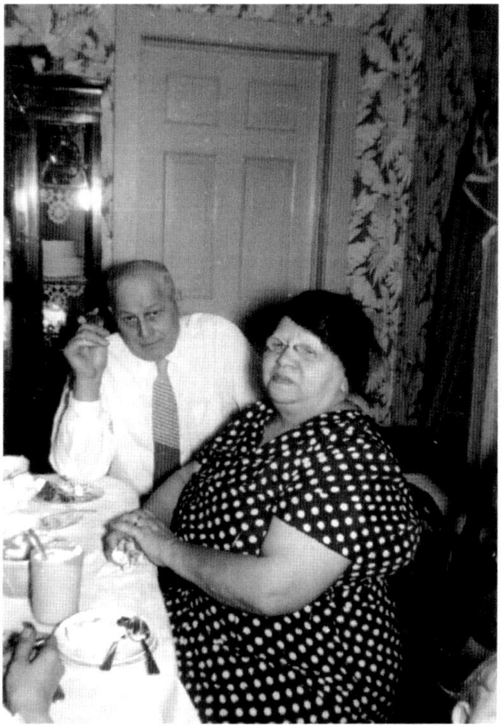

Josephine and Michael Wytrwal at Christmas, 1950. *Stanley Zurawel.*

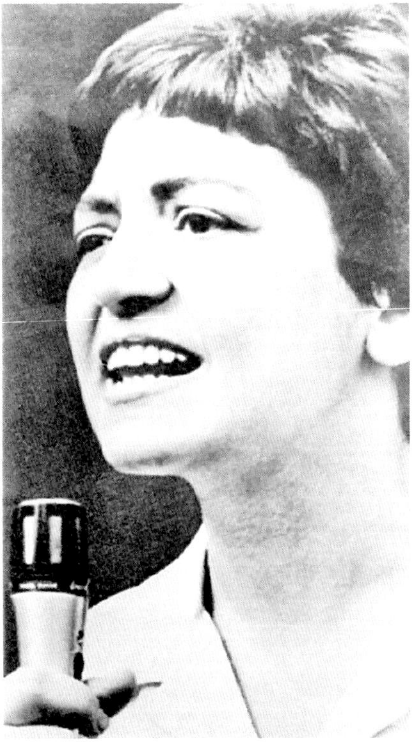

Amsterdam native Mary Anne Krupsak when she was New York lieutenant governor. *Leader Herald.*

When he died on January 21, 1970, the *Recorder* editorialized that Wytrwal was "likeable, friendly, considerate, a progressive in the finest sense of the word."

After Wytrwal's death, Krupsak won a state senate seat. She was elected lieutenant governor in 1974, running with Democrat Hugh Carey. In 1978, she unsuccessfully challenged Carey for governor in a Democratic primary.

After leaving public life, she worked as an attorney, encouraging startup companies. The work was similar to what her grandfather had done in Amsterdam, where he negotiated deals to help the community with nothing more than a handshake.

"People trusted him because of his honor," Krupsak said.

Polish National Legion

The Polish National Legion (PNL) was one of several Polish fraternal organizations during Amsterdam's industrial heyday. The organization had a military purpose when founded as the Polish Legion in 1909, stressing military readiness with the goal of assisting in defense of the Polish homeland.

The first legion captain was Peter Wolak, a veteran of U.S. Army campaigns in the Philippines. Captain Wolak led military drills, and the legion was reported to be a well-trained unit that "compared well to the regular army."

In 1915, members decided to offer a civilian program for those not interested or not able to join the military unit. The organization's name was changed to the Polish National Legion, and land was purchased on Vanderveer Street for a PNL home.

In World War I, about half the members enlisted either in the American or Polish army. Poland was liberated after the war. After the war, Legion formed a bowling league and also had baseball and softball teams.

The organization created a PNL men's glee club in 1946, a singing group that performed throughout the area. In 1953, Stanley Slusarz was glee club director when that year's member portrait was taken. Tom Czelusniak, who was active in politics and a pigeon fancier, was president.

When the organization closed its doors in the 1980s, each member received a share of the PNL's remaining fund balance.

More than a Waitress

When Orsini's Royal Restaurant at East Main and Liberty Streets in Amsterdam opened in the 1920s, there were curtains on the booths. Customers who were not Italian "didn't quite know how to eat spaghetti," according to a family member. Those patrons who were embarrassed to be seen eating this strange ethnic dish closed the curtains when dining on pasta. The Board of Health eventually ordered the curtains removed.

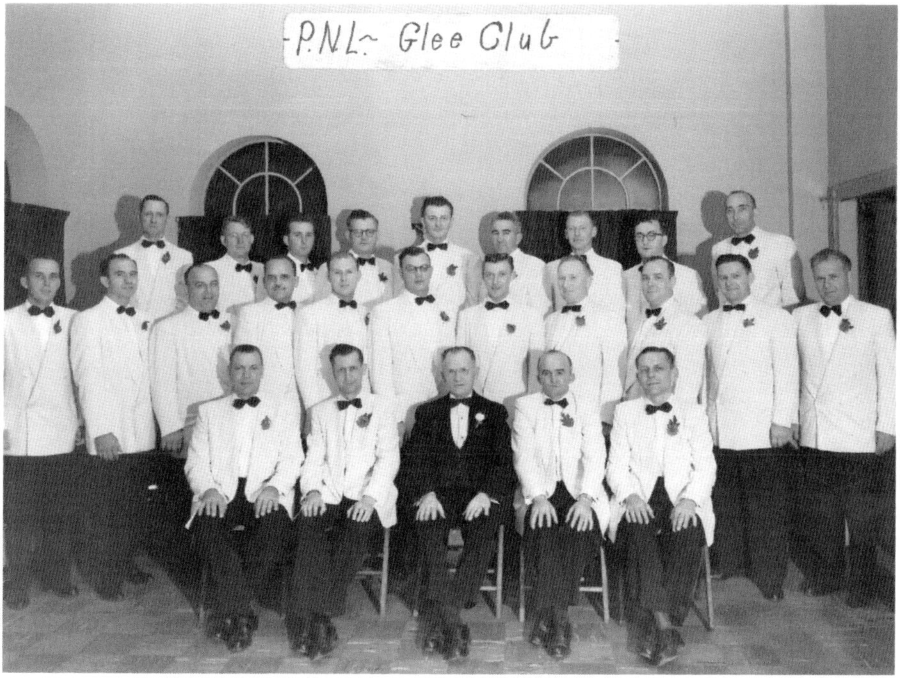

The director of the Polish National Legion's glee club, Stanley Slusarz, wore a black jacket in 1953. To his left is club president Tom Czelusniak. *David Dybas.*

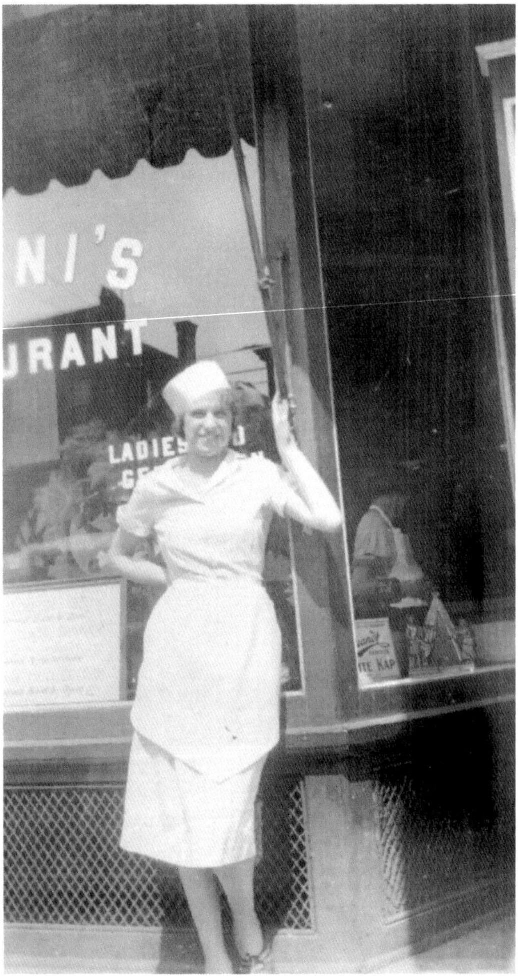

Genevieve Orsini outside her family's Amsterdam restaurant. *Genevieve Palombo.*

Anthony Orsini, an immigrant from Abruzzi, and his wife, Julia Richitelli, born near Naples, started the restaurant—also known as the Royal Lunch—after Anthony learned cooking at Amsterdam's diners. It was a family business involving sons Ralph, Arthur and Alfred and daughters Mary and Genevieve.

Genevieve Orsini Hartigan Palombo turned ninety-seven this year and enjoys her family, which today includes daughter Jennifer Ziskin; stepdaughters Carol Natale and Sandra Mockry; seven granddaughters; and five great-grandchildren.

Palombo grew up in Amsterdam and was a founder of Psi Chi Phi, a high school club for Italian girls.

After graduating from high school, Palombo worked as a waitress at Orsini's: "We had to wear an apron. We had to wear a decent-looking outfit. And we had to be very neat. We had the pencil on a chain."

Ten cents was a usual tip, and then twenty-five cents became standard. Waitress Sonie Perillo, who now lives in Florida, "found fifty cents on the table one time and she was really surprised."

When retired judge Robert Sise was a youth, he was among youngsters who went to first Friday communion at St. Mary's Church and then stopped at Orsini's for breakfast before school. The parents gave the children money and told Palombo to supervise. Sise wanted a chocolate doughnut, but

Palombo made him have toast or oatmeal. "Bob was a little annoyed with me," Palombo said.

Richard Ellers, who now lives in Ohio, remembers the Orsini meal ticket. Waitresses punched the ticket, which cost $4.50 but was worth $5.00 in food. During the Depression, Orsini's offered a blue-plate special, and one of Palombo's current neighbors on Amsterdam's Pleasant Avenue still has one of the blue plates. The special cost thirty-five cents and featured meat or fish, mashed potatoes and vegetables. Coffee was an extra five cents.

The Strand Theater was across the street, and stage performers such as Baby Rose Marie and Buddy Ebsen frequented Orsini's Royal Restaurant.

In the early 1940s, Anthony Orsini relocated to Market Street, next to Montgomery County Trust. The new facility was named Orsini's Restaurant. It was open twenty-four hours a day, with young Ralph Orsini handling the overnight shift. There was more room for wedding receptions; a six-course Italian meal cost one dollar a plate.

Genevieve Orsini married Edward Hartigan in 1944. Hartigan fought with Merrill's Marauders in the China-Burma-India Theater in World War II. He had been a vaudeville performer and bartender and later worked at the Scotia Naval Depot. He died in 1964. The Hartigans had two children, Michael and Jennifer. Michael died in 1984. The Hartigans lived at the corner of Division and Pine Streets and took in boarders, including members of the Rugmakers baseball team and WCSS radio announcers.

Orsini's Restaurant closed in the mid-1950s. Anthony Orsini then worked as a cook for Tony Griffin at the Wil-Ton Lanes on Main Street. Later, his son Ralph opened an Orsini's eatery on Wall Street near the former junior high school, where students bought the best French fries in town in little paper bags.

After Orsini's closed on Market Street, Palombo waited on tables at Isabel's on West Main Street and was a waitress for Pedro Perez at the Elks Club and a lakeside restaurant. In 1957, she began working for the New York Retirement System, retiring herself in 1974. That year, she married Morris Palombo, a widower who was a food broker. He died in 1999.

Keep Cool at Duchessi's

Duchessi's Importing Company was such an important part of downtown Amsterdam in the late 1940s that proprietor Peter Duchessi started a summer fashion trend.

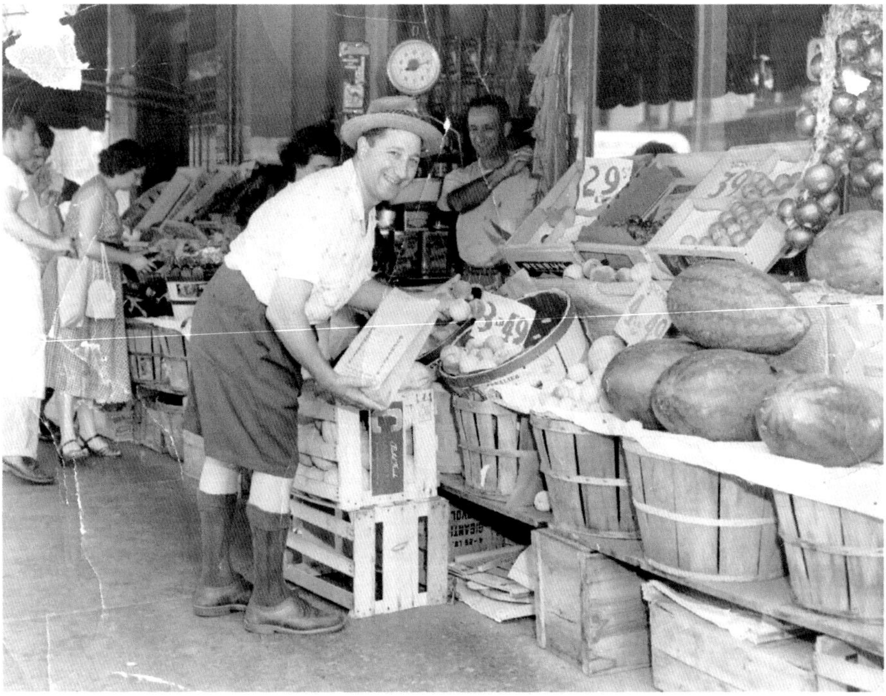

Peter Duchessi introduced shorts as a fashion item for downtown Amsterdam shopkeepers in the 1940s. *Peter Duchessi.*

Duchessi was pictured in the local paper wearing shorts as he tended to peaches and cantaloupes arrayed in bins in front of his store. The caption read, "Keep cool at Duchessi's." Later, H. Mortan Guttenberg, proprietor of Mortan's men's store, thanked Duchessi for helping start a run on men's shorts.

Duchessi, son of Mariano and Maria Padovani Duchessi, is part of a local family who also produced the head of a national veteran's organization, an Amsterdam mayor and a national union leader.

When Peter Duchessi was born in 1917, the family lived on the South Side. They moved across the river to Knollwood Avenue on Henrietta Heights when he was eleven. They were one of the few Italian families in the neighborhood.

Times were tough in the Depression, and young Duchessi left school to work mowing lawns for the wealthy on nearby Guy Park Avenue for twenty-five cents each. He sold flowers and apples outside a silk mill.

Boxing Brothers

In 1935, much to his mother's chagrin, Peter Duchessi started boxing and became the first member of the family to use the nickname "Duke." He was known for endurance, courage, speed and a powerful left hook. He is proud that he was able to go six rounds against future champ Sugar Ray Robinson. He fought seventy-one fights and had fifty-seven victories, fifteen of them knockouts.

Peter's younger brother, the late John Duchessi Sr., also became a boxer, winning sixteen of his seventeen fights. John Sr., known as "Duke the Dropper," slugged his way to a decision over Don Trott of Saratoga Springs in a pioneer televised boxing match on WRGB in Schenectady in 1942.

Inducted into the army combat engineers, John Sr. was badly wounded in the Battle of Monte Cassino, Italy, and the recipient of the Purple Heart. After the war, he married Eleanor Zappone and worked with another brother, Anthony Duchessi, at Anthony's Church Street meat market.

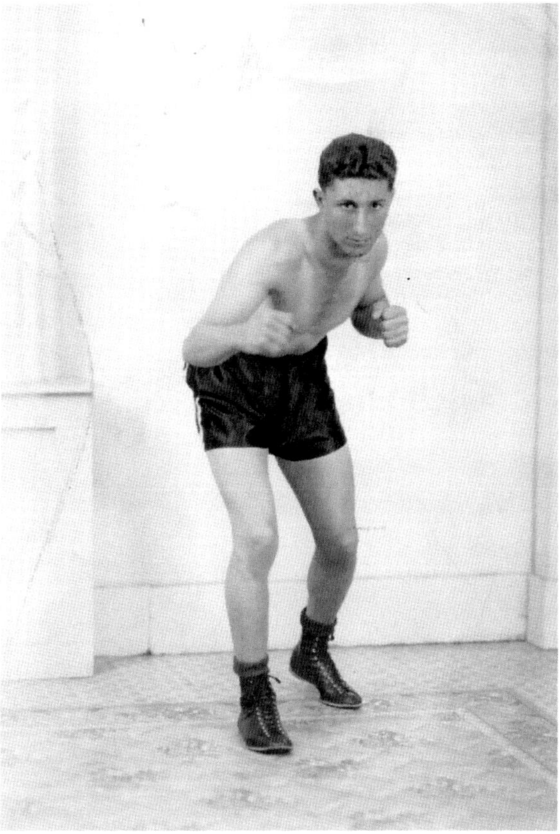

Peter "Duke" Duchessi won fifty-seven of seventy-one fights. *Peter Duchessi.*

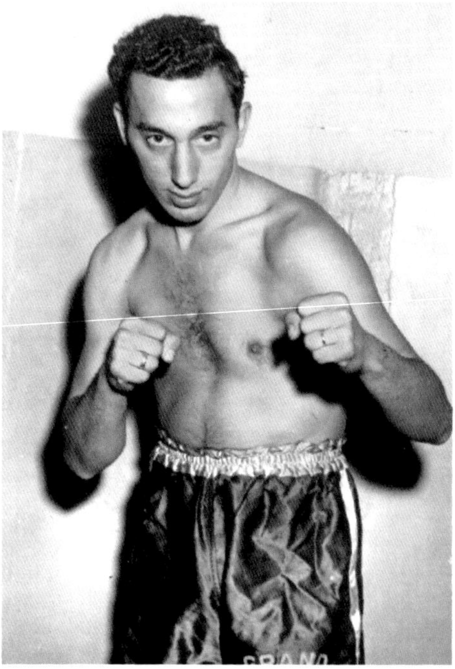

John "Duke the Dropper" Duchessi Sr. won sixteen of seventeen fights. *Duchessi family.*

William, yet another Duchessi brother, became a local and then national officer of the union that represented Amsterdam's carpet mill workers: the Textile Workers Union of America. William Duchessi died in 1979.

John Sr. became national commander of the Military Order of the Purple Heart in the 1970s. One of his sons, John Duchessi Jr., was elected mayor of Amsterdam from 1996 through 2003. John Sr. died in 2008.

The Import Business

Peter Duchessi worked long hours for five dollars a week at Home Dairy Cafeteria and then at Bigelow Sanford in Amsterdam at the end of the Depression. Not able to serve in the armed forces because of injuries from an auto accident, he was employed at American Locomotive in Schenectady welding plates for gun carriers.

He married Madeline Lanzi of Amsterdam's famous South Side restaurant family but was laid off by Alco at war's end. With help from his wife's uncle, Ralph Marotta, he started Duchessi's Importing Company, located at 128 East Main Street.

His store was among the first in the area to stock imported olive oil, pasta, cheeses, vegetables and fruits from Italy and elsewhere, even oranges from Israel. His customers came from all ethnic groups and economic strata, including the wealthy, who insisted on personal service from Duchessi himself.

His was the last store to close when downtown was torn down to make way for the shopping mall that was built in the 1970s. Duchessi bought Dean's Market on Lincoln Avenue on Market Hill and moved his importing company there until he closed the store in 1981.

He later worked at Price Chopper Supermarkets, where he introduced the concept of the custom-cut meat department. Although he retired in 1982, he still demonstrates new food products at Price Chopper on Route 30 in Amsterdam.

He and his wife live on Brookside Avenue. Their son is University at Albany professor Dr. Peter Duchessi of Ballston Spa, and their daughter is retired teacher Linda Meenan of Glenville.

The DiMezza Bank

An Italian American family once operated the DiMezza Bank in Amsterdam. Pasquale DiMezza, a native of Melizanno in Benevento Province, also published an Italian newspaper and sold real estate and products ranging from steamship tickets to macaroni.

DiMezza even wanted to erect a merry-go-round in 1908 on Railroad Street, a project humorously deplored by the *Recorder* newspaper, whose offices were nearby: "It is sincerely hoped that some natural phenomenon destroys the aforesaid music before the first shrill blast of the whistle stuns the fish in the river."

DiMezza opened his bank at 40 Bridge Street on the South Side and was the victim of a violent attack there on July 16, 1914. A man entered the business about 9:00 p.m. asking for a postage stamp. DiMezza, engaged in conversation with a friend, directed the stranger to his wife, Carmela, who was standing behind a counter. The man then pulled out a knife or razor, slashed DiMezza's face and fled. A bleeding DiMezza gave chase but couldn't catch his assailant.

Police officer William Conrad joined the pursuit and drew his revolver but was afraid to shoot as a crowd of women and children had appeared because of the commotion. Conrad fired at the fleeing man as the chase continued past the Minaville Street bridge over the Erie Canal. The suspect disappeared down the West Shore Railroad tracks toward Schenectady.

Meanwhile, DiMezza had summoned a Dr. Canna to treat the two-and-a-half-inch gash and notified police headquarters. The *Recorder* speculated that the attack was meant to be an act of vengeance that would live on in the scar that would be visible on DiMezza's face.

DiMezza may have been targeted for taking a statement for authorities from an Italian-speaking man sentenced to prison in a previous slashing attack. And DiMezza had been a witness in the federal prosecution of a man who had been passing counterfeit Italian and other foreign currency at the DiMezza Bank and other institutions.

Two months after the attack, a suspect, Umberto Vinci, was arrested in Brooklyn. Fortunato Machri of the New York Central detectives of Albany

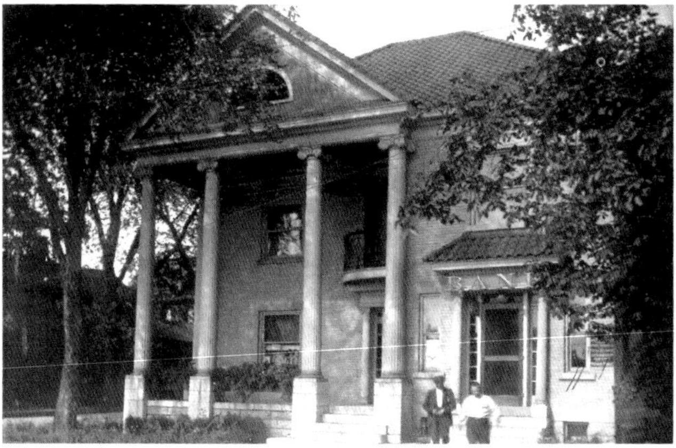

The DiMezza Bank at 75 West Main Street in Amsterdam. *Montgomery County Department of History and Archives.*

had been working on the case and brought Vinci to Amsterdam. Vinci was identified as the assailant by the DiMezzas and other witnesses but protested his innocence. He also had a facial scar, said to be a mark of the criminal organization the Black Hand.

Vinci was found not guilty in court in Fonda on March 25, 1915. His attorney, Clark Jordan of New York City, introduced witnesses who testified that Vinci was working at a shoe factory in Brooklyn on the day of the attack. One man testified he had shaved Vinci in Brooklyn that day.

The *Recorder* wrote, "That the assailant of Mr. DiMezza, who is a leader among his fellow countrymen and a reputable citizen, has not been made to suffer the penalty of his crime is generally deplored."

In 1916, DiMezza relocated his bank and his home across the river to 75 West Main Street at the corner of Mohawk Place. When DiMezza closed the bank in 1930, state examiners said his adherence to state banking laws had been perfect. He was known for serving customers at any hour of the day or night.

When Prohibition was repealed, the business became a liquor store that was operated by Pasquale DiMezza's son Alphonse starting in 1945. Hundreds paid their respects when Pasquale DiMezza, at age seventy-five, died in January 1947. The 75 Main Street building was torn down for urban renewal highway work in 1966.

Amsterdam town supervisor Thomas Pasquale DiMezza, retired detective lieutenant in the Amsterdam city police department, is a grandson of banker Pasquale DiMezza.

Officer Nelson—Big, Gruff but Nice

An Amsterdam police officer is well remembered by relatives and former Guy Park Avenue elementary school students. Andrew C. Nelson was born in Amsterdam in 1893, the son of Andrew and Minnie Coons Nelson. He attended West Spring Street School and lived in the West End most of his life. He served in the navy in World War I. After the war, he worked at Bigelow-Sanford carpet mill. He married Edith Townsend of Tribes Hill in 1926.

In 1927, Nelson became a member of the city police force. Before switching to driving a police car late in his career, Officer Nelson rode police motorcycles. One of the cycles that Nelson used was a three-wheeler; another had a sidecar.

Nelson's niece Florence Orlando, now of Gloversville, recalled that her aunt and uncle came to visit her family in Mount Kisco, New York, with Andy in the driver's seat of an Indian motorcycle and Edith behind him. Orlando still has Nelson's nightstick. Orlando recalled that people said Officer Nelson would give his own mother a traffic ticket. He once attached a ticket to a car owned by the police chief, illegally parked near the chief's home.

Orlando said, "He was a big man, very gruff. You listened to him when he talked and were kind of scared of him. But he wasn't going to harm you."

Nelson protected children crossing Guy Park Avenue to get to the elementary school. One of those children was Peter Betz, who now lives in Perth. Betz, Fulton County historian, said Nelson once arrested a yo-yo salesman at Guy Park Avenue School. He also once tamed a gray squirrel to eat from his hand for the amusement of the children.

Guy Park alumnus Lawrence Spagnola lived near the Nelsons on Carmichael Street. Spagnola said neighborhood kids played football in front of Nelson's home, but he never chased them away.

"I don't like admitting that from time to time we actually challenged him," Spagnola said. "He was always understanding and just knew that it was nothing personal, and he understood that we didn't mean anything against him."

Amsterdam native Eugene Leonard of Garden Grove, California, said Nelson was a father figure who made sure he played it straight. One day, Leonard questioned the accuracy of the speedometer on his car. Officer Nelson proposed a test. Leonard set off down Guy Park Avenue with his window open and Nelson followed on his motorcycle yelling out instructions, such as "Bring it up to thirty miles per hour!" Leonard was sure people thought he was a miscreant being pursued by the diligent cop.

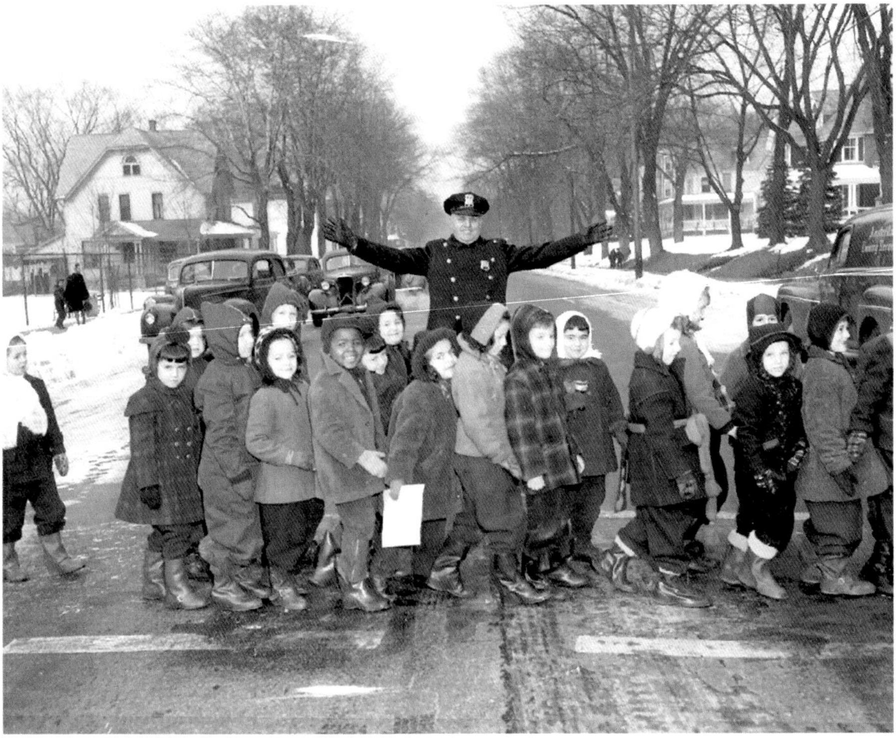

Officer Andy Nelson doing school traffic duty in the 1940s in Amsterdam. *Montgomery County Department of History and Archives.*

Nelson's brother-in-law, Louis Townsend of Fort Johnson, said Nelson was very strict on the police force but in reality was a gentle man who loved children. Nelson and his wife had no children of their own. He enjoyed holidays and sometimes played Santa Claus.

Nelson retired in 1958 and enjoyed hunting and especially fishing in his retirement, often accompanied by his wife. He died in 1965 while on a fishing trip at Lake Pleasant. He and his wife were Methodists who worshipped at churches in Tribes Hill and Division Street in Amsterdam.

His obituary stated, "Assigned to enforce the Motor Vehicle Law in the days prior to tire-screeching, mufflerless and public thoroughfare drag racing, Nelson was considered a tough cop who knew the law and enforced it without regard to his personal welfare."

Recorder police reporter Wallace McBride Kimball once said if the city had four officers like Andy Nelson and Stanley Bush, another highly regarded Amsterdam cop, the rest of the police force could be dismissed.

The Wars and the Warriors

Civil War

The 115th

The author of a book called *The 115th New York in the Civil War* believes that the local volunteer unit was nicknamed the "Iron Hearted Regiment" after the war. Mark Silo of Loudonville is a civil engineer with the State Department of Transportation whose avocation is Civil War history.

In 1865, a regiment member from Clifton Park wrote a history of the 115th entitled *The Iron Hearted Regiment*. "That sounded great, but in the course of my research, no one in the war used that phrase," Silo said. He believes the author or editor simply created the title.

The regiment went to war from Fonda. The men from Montgomery, Fulton and Saratoga Counties had responded to President Abraham Lincoln's call for 300,000 volunteers in the summer of 1862. The local area met its quota in one month.

The men gathered in a field north of Fonda called Camp Mohawk. For years, there was a Camp Mohawk Motel, but now the field is mostly vacant.

Reaching Baltimore, Maryland, by train, the men encountered hostility marching from one train to another in that city, which had a large share of Southern sympathizers.

Within two weeks of leaving Fonda, the 115th took part in the Battle of Harpers Ferry, Virginia, now West Virginia. They were among a group of eleven thousand soldiers surrendered by a Union general as the battle began.

"The men were mortified to be surrendered without a fight," Silo said. Ironically, the general who ordered the surrender died in the Rebel bombardment before the Confederates saw the Union white flags.

"In those days, they used an honor system for prisoners of war," Silo said. "They pledged not to fight against the Confederacy until they were officially exchanged, which happened a few months later."

The 115th was held in Union custody in Chicago. As they boarded their train for Washington to join the war, their Chicago barracks caught fire. A trial was held in their absence, and the 115th was found guilty of arson, although Silo said records at the National Archives do not confirm their guilt. The Mohawk Valley soldiers were banished to perform manual labor for a year in Hilton Head, South Carolina.

When the 115th finally did get into combat, it was brutal. Half of the six-hundred-man regiment was killed or wounded in the Battle of Olustee, Florida. In all, four hundred members of the 115th died during the war, many from disease.

Their first commander, Colonel Simeon Sammons, was wounded in the foot at Olustee. Sammons recovered but was wounded again when the regiment fought at the Crater in Petersburg, Virginia. Sammons returned to Fonda and later was elected to the state legislature. Silo said the remains of Sammons's home still can be seen on Route 30A in Fonda.

Silo said the Florida campaign of 1864 was political in origin. Supporters of the idea convinced President Lincoln that they could get Florida back into the

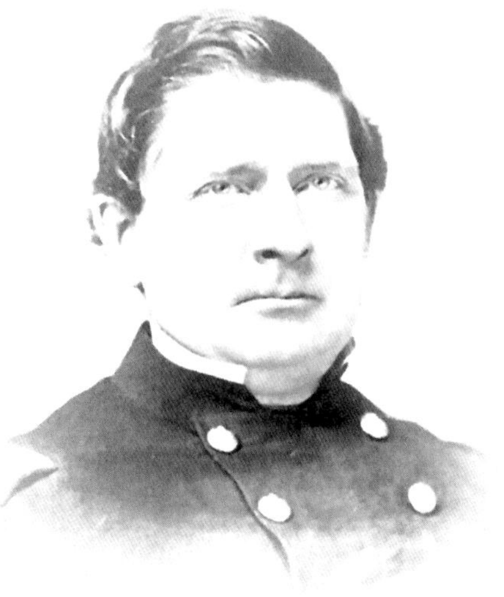

Colonel Simeon Sammons of Fonda, commander of the 115th New York regiment in the Civil War. *Mark Silo.*

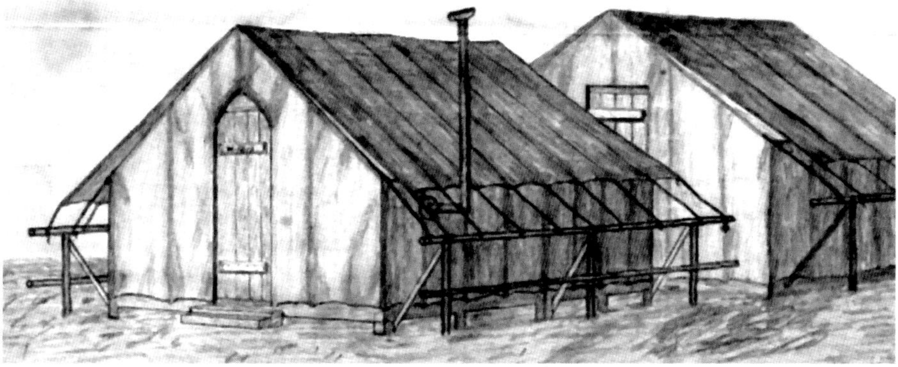

Colonel Sammons's headquarters tent at Hilton Head, an illustration he sent home to his family. *Mark Silo.*

Union. The Union managed to occupy the Jacksonville area for the rest of the war, but Silo said the Florida campaign didn't amount to much strategically.

Silo's book has attracted more than customary interest because it deals with lesser-known battles. "There are a lot of histories written of individual regiments, and most of them cover the same ground over and over," Silo said. "Bull Run, Gettysburg that kind of thing. These guys from the Mohawk Valley fought in Olustee, Florida and Fort Fisher, North Carolina."

Silo found out about the 115th because of his mother-in-law, who lives in St. Johnsville. He had bought her a late nineteenth-century book that contained an engraving of her great-grandfather's farm in Palatine Bridge. There was a story about the 115th New York in that book. For Silo, the rest was history.

Medal of Honor

A Canajoharie man was awarded the Congressional Medal of Honor for his actions at the Battle of Petersburg, Virginia, in April 1865. Frank Shubert was a sergeant with Company E of the Forty-third New York Infantry. Shubert was born in Germany in 1841 and died in 1920. He is buried at Canajoharie's Prospect Hill Cemetery.

In the battle, Shubert captured two Confederate markers. A postwar directory listed Shubert as a manufacturer and dealer in boots and shoes with his partner, Christopher Sticht.

"I came across Frank Shubert [Franz Joubert] when researching my genealogy," said Ed Archinal of Amsterdam. "He was the brother of my great-grandmother. The store he sold shoes from still stands [on Church Street] in Canajoharie."

A document at the county archives indicated that Shubert made $10,000 per year, making him one of the leading businessmen in Canajoharie. Shubert's daughter, Bertelle, married Edward W. Shineman, chairman of the board of Beech-Nut in Canajoharie from 1948 to 1954.

Funeral Train

The Civil War and assassination of President Abraham Lincoln helped shape the funeral customs we follow today. Embalming became popular during the war as a way to preserve bodies killed in battle that had to be transported hundreds of miles home. When Lincoln was shot, his body was embalmed and went on its long final journey back to Illinois by train, including a stop in Amsterdam at 5:25 p.m. on April 26, 1865.

The funeral train was tremendous publicity for the effectiveness of embalming. Amsterdam woodworker Isaac S. Shuler had started making coffins in 1862, and after the Civil War, he began offering undertaking services.

When Shuler died, his undertaking business was operated by a pillar of Amsterdam society and culture: W. Max Reid. Reid is known as a historian for his 1901 book *The Mohawk Valley*. Undertaker Reid was also president of the business-boosting Amsterdam Board of Trade from its founding in 1884 until 1901. Reid died in 1911, and his estate ran the business until 1913.

In 1913, Raymond Johnson and Edwin H. Lindsay purchased the firm, naming it Johnson & Lindsay. Lindsay died in 1930, but the name remained. At first located on West Main near Pine Street, the business had moved to 11 Mohawk Place by the early 1930s.

Johnson locally pioneered moving funerals from the home to the funeral parlor in the 1930s, according to Vincent Rossi. Rossi is a principal in the firm that is the successor to Johnson & Lindsay: Betz, Rossi, Bellinger and Stewart Family Funeral Home with facilities in Amsterdam, Broadalbin, Fultonville, Canajoharie and Gloversville.

Amsterdam's Armory

The architect of the National Guard armory on Florida Avenue on Amsterdam's South Side designed twenty-six other Upstate armories, including structures on Washington Avenue in Albany and in Saratoga Springs.

Isaac Perry earned his reputation for creating impressive public buildings when he built the New York State Inebriate Asylum in Binghamton in 1857. Self-taught, Perry in effect became the state's official architect. He was selected by Governor Grover Cleveland in the 1880s to get the massive project of building the state capitol in Albany back on track.

According to Nancy L. Todd's book *New York's Historic Armories*, the Amsterdam armory was built in 1895, initially to house the 46th Separate Company of the National Guard, which became Company G of the 105th Infantry Regiment three years later. Todd, an architectural historian, is a program analyst with the New York State Office of Parks, Recreation and Historic Preservation.

Armories were built in numerous states, according to Todd, to house units of the National Guard, the backbone of the American military until World War I. The state-controlled units were composed of local men who needed training space. The heyday of armory construction was in the late nineteenth and early twentieth centuries.

Todd said, "In some of the bigger cities during the era of labor-capital conflict, the armories were also built to be monuments to law and order

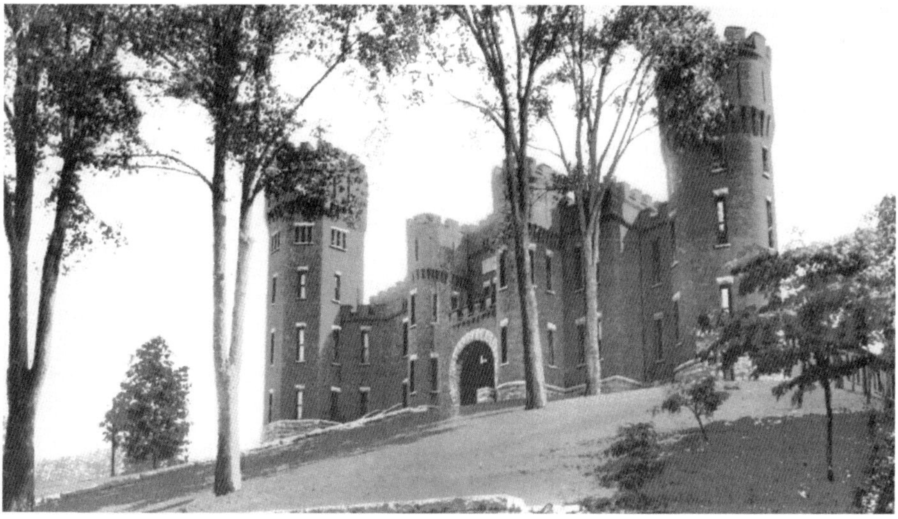

A postcard view of the Amsterdam Armory, 1905. *Bob Cudmore.*

and the American way of life and to look like imposing castles and military facilities."

The middle and upper classes, Todd said, feared the new wave of Eastern European immigrants, some of whom espoused socialism, Communism and even anarchy. In New York City, huge armories were built, according to Todd, to inspire fear and awe.

Upstate, fears of class warfare were not intense, and armories were built more as expressions of grand, state-funded improvements for local communities.

According to historian Hugh Donlon, the state told Amsterdam officials in 1888 to provide the National Guard with drilling and training facilities. For four years, troops drilled on the top floor of the Behr Building on Main Street, at a cost of $700 a year to the city. The state ultimately came through with $45,000 to build the armory on land previously owned by a family named Devendorf. The hilltop site gives the imposing structure a great view and a commanding presence overlooking the city.

Armories became what Todd called luxurious clubhouses for National Guard members, which helped with recruiting. And since National Guard members lived in the community, armories were used for trade shows, political rallies and sporting events such as basketball—and, in Amsterdam's case, even roller polo.

There was a serious side. Jean Rogers Wilson of Amsterdam recalled that her father, Lieutenant Colonel Peter J. Rogers, was a member of the National Guard all his adult life.

Wilson remembered the day that Company G left by train for World War II: "So many of those young men did not return from the war, but I can still see their faces and the pride they had in the company and my dad's love for each one of them."

Todd said some of the state's one hundred armories are still used by the National Guard, but many are now owned by their communities or nonprofit organizations.

The thirty-six-thousand-square-foot Amsterdam armory, according to Todd, is the only in the state that is a private residence. The armory was sold to the Diana family in 1994 and purchased in 2005 by Susan and Manfred Phemister, who live in the building and continue to renovate it. The building has been the scene of movie shoots, and the Phemisters have rented the drill shed and an elegant upstairs room for social events. They call the structure Amsterdam Castle and operate a thriving bed-and-breakfast in it.

The Roughneck and the Cook

Fear of enemy attack on vital transportation links is not new. According to Craig Williams of the New York State Archives in Albany, soldiers guarded the entire state canal system and railroad network in World War I and World War II.

In World War I, Margaret Cook, my grandmother, fed soldiers who guarded Lock 13 on the Mohawk River/Barge Canal. She lived on the south side of the waterway in Randall, along what is today Route 5S. The soldiers were stationed north of the canal at Yosts.

When built in the nineteenth century, the Erie Canal was a man-made ditch. In a major reconstruction project that began in 1903, the canal in the eastern Mohawk Valley was moved so that it followed the course of the Mohawk River.

My grandmother was a newcomer to Randall. Born in the Catskill Mountain hamlet of Chichester, near Phoenicia, in 1873, Margaret was married twice. Her first marriage produced one son but ended in divorce in Brooklyn, where her husband, John Haas, was a carpenter.

In 1909, at age thirty-six, she married Yates Cook, fifty-seven, and moved to Randall, where her new husband was a pillar of the community and the church and managed the local store. The year before, Yates Cook's first wife, also named Margaret, had been killed when hit by a freight train near the passenger station in Fultonville on the West Shore line.

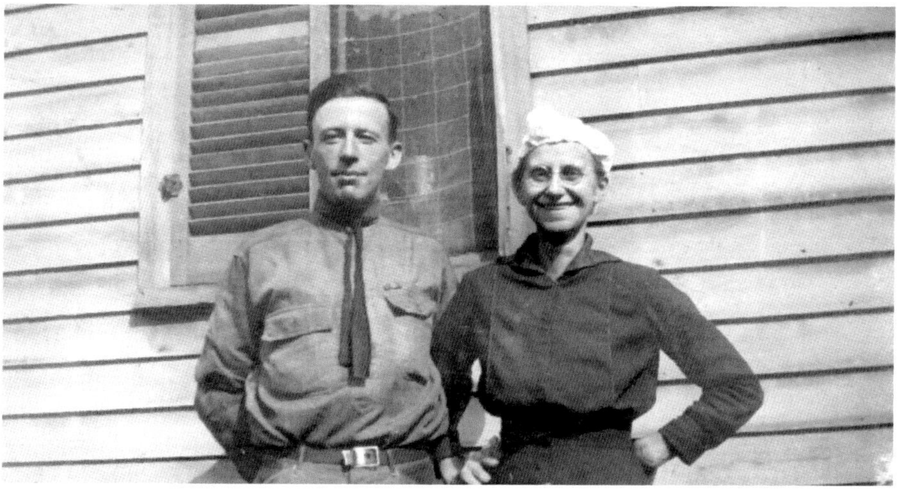

Roughneck was one of the soldiers guarding the Barge Canal lock in Randall in World War I. Margaret Cook fed the soldiers. *Bob Cudmore.*

Yates and my grandmother had three children in quick succession, the last being my mother, Julia, born in 1913. Yates died in 1915, from what was described as a ruptured blood vessel as he hitched up a horse and wagon for a trip to Fonda.

The outbreak of war and the need to feed soldiers guarding the canal made it financially feasible for my grandmother and her children to remain in Randall for the duration of the war.

She left behind a photo album that was made by one of those soldiers. There are several pictures of her with individual soldiers. Margaret Cook was a cook by name and nature, and the captions all used the word "Cook" to describe her: "Cook and the Midnight Mechanic," "Cook and the Loafer" and "The Roughneck and the Cook."

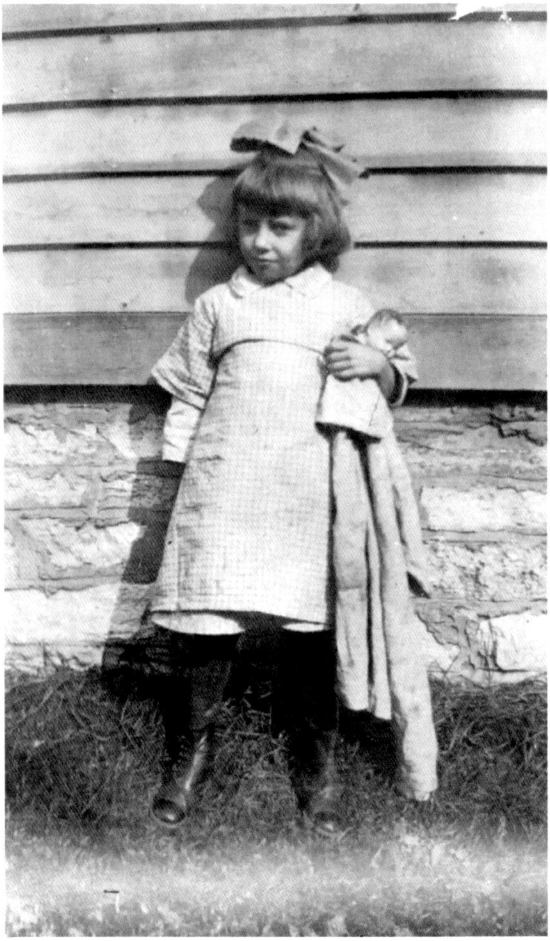

Julia was Margaret Cook's youngest daughter and author Bob Cudmore's mother. *Bob Cudmore.*

Young women appear in several photos, and in one, captioned "Sis," a woman is holding a rifle and is wearing a soldier's coat. A man in uniform is shown with an umbrella over his shoulder, and the caption reads, "The Sissy." My mother's photo caption is: "Julia—the queen of Randall."

One of my grandmother's "boys" is identified because of a clipping pasted in the photo album from a newspaper called the *Saturday Globe*, dated November 22, 1917.

The headline states: "Real patriotism: Mrs. Cook expresses her feelings in deeds not words." The article quotes Private William J. Allen of Fonda, a member of Company C, Second Regiment, New York Infantry, "one of the guards of barge canal lock 13."

> *Private Allen writes that Mrs. Cook is a widow with three small children. She has been cook for the boys at Yosts since the war broke out and 14 of "her boys" are in France and seven more are in training camps. She has mothered them all and the boys look to her for smiles and other necessities as well as for their meals.*

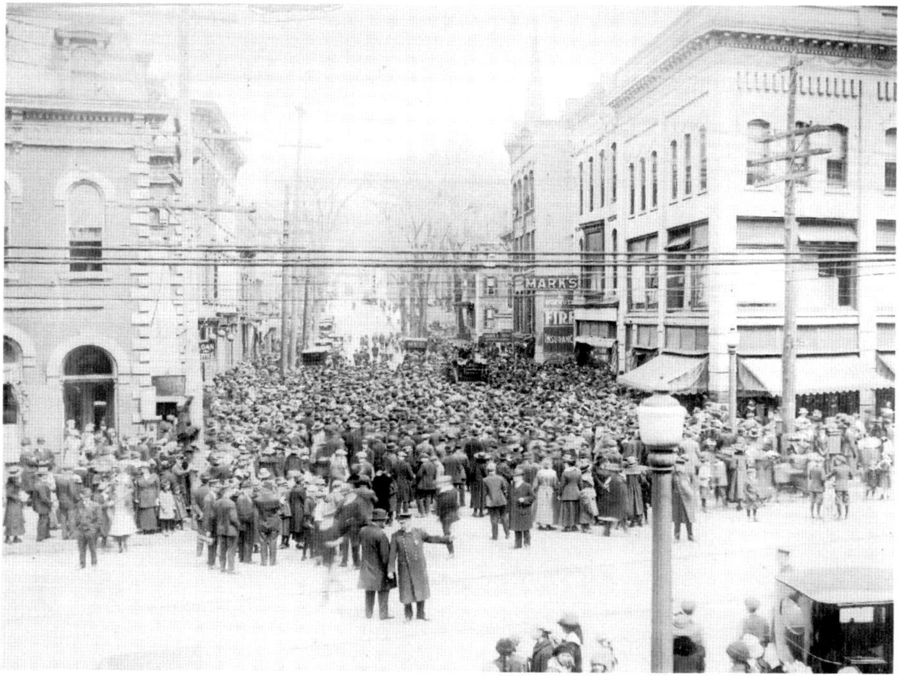

A World War I bond drive in downtown Amsterdam. *Montgomery County Department of History and Archives.*

> *Mrs. Cook has seven Liberty Bonds and is buying* [war stamps]. *She asks for her change in Thrift Stamps of which she has several books. The boys in France who have boarded with her she does not forget but sends them cigarettes or money to buy them. She is now sending Christmas gifts. Her constant thought is to keep the boys happy and contented with army life. Private Allen wishes there were more who would buy bonds and help the government to bring the boys back to America.*

When the war ended in 1918, Margaret Cook and her children moved to Amsterdam where she continued cooking--running a boarding house at 107½ Forbes Street in the East End. She lived with us when I was young and used to make me bread and jam every night before I went to bed. She died in 1953 at age 80.

GUADALCANAL DIARY

"When I was in the South Pacific, I dreamed of getting home," Sergeant Joseph A. Bucci told a gathering at a testimonial dinner in his native Amsterdam in 1943. "Just at the present, I wish I were down there again."

Bucci had been awarded the Silver Star for his heroism during the Battle of Matinuku River on Guadalcanal in 1942. He was the son of Charles and Mary Bucci, who lived at 12 Lark Street in the East End. Charles Bucci had served in World War I. Another son, Anthony, served in the Army Air Corps in World War II.

Joseph Bucci was a graduate of St. Mary's Institute and the University of Notre Dame. He came back home to work as a life insurance agent for John Hancock. After the attack on Pearl Harbor, he was among the first local youths to enlist as a private in the U.S. Marines on January 26, 1942.

By October, he was fighting the Japanese on Guadalcanal Island in the Pacific and found himself and six others pinned down by Japanese artillery fire near Matiniku River. The small band had missed orders to move from their foxholes to another position.

Through one long night and the next day, the seven endured a Japanese artillery barrage and attack. The seven marines were credited with killing 175 to 200 Japanese soldiers. Then, Bucci and his comrades came under American artillery fire in a marine counter attack. Ultimately, the seven marines were reunited with their unit.

That November, Bucci was wounded by three pieces of shrapnel. He contracted malaria and was shipped to a military hospital in San Diego, California.

It was there that he learned he was to receive the Silver Star and Purple Heart for his actions on Guadalcanal. He was promoted to sergeant.

Bucci was home on leave in July 1943 when the *Recorder* printed an account of his actions on Guadalcanal written by marine private Eddie Lyon, who had interviewed Bucci at the San Diego hospital. Bucci and his parents went to the *Recorder* offices to get their first look at the news story and to have their pictures taken.

In December 1943, Bucci was still at home, assigned to the Scotia Naval Depot on Route 5, today an industrial park. He had applied for Officer Candidate School.

That month, Knights of Columbus Council 209 in Amsterdam honored Bucci at a dinner at the then Amsterdam Hotel on East Main Street and presented him with a special ring. Bucci spoke at numerous gatherings while home on leave on behalf of the war effort.

He told the Knights of Columbus, "It is my fond wish and hope that this international mess will soon be over and that all of us can come back to the good old American way of life. However, I expect to be shoving off again soon, and in whatever part of the world I am, I will have this ring with me—a reminder of your thoughtfulness, and I will be thoughtful for you."

Bucci went to Officer Candidate School and became a second lieutenant in October 1944. A 1951 clipping states that Bucci was promoted to captain in the Marine Corps Reserve by President Truman. Bucci was studying at Albany Law School at the time.

His widow, Louanne Wilkes Bucci, is an Albany native. She said the two met when Bucci was at Albany Law. He did not become a lawyer but became a probation officer. In the 1950s, the Buccis relocated to Grass Valley, California, where Bucci worked for Ventura County until his retirement.

In recent years, the elder Buccis moved to Arrington, Virginia, to the home of their son. Bucci, ninety-six, died on February 8, 2010. Inurnment took place at Arlington National Cemetery.

Townsends, Watroba, Haas

Five sons and one son-in-law of Louis G. Townsend Sr. and his wife, Sarah Beyer Townsend of Tribes Hill, served in the U.S. Army in World War II. All survived the war.

There were eleven Townsend children: six boys and five girls. Their father worked as an inspector at Bigelow Sanford Carpet Company. The family home in Tribes Hill was on what was called Railroad Avenue and later called Thompson Avenue. They were near the railroad tracks on the way to the river bridge leading to Fort Hunter. The building was destroyed by fire after the Townsends left the structure.

The first Townsend to enter military service was William, inducted in January 1941. He was sent home that November. The Japanese attacked Pearl Harbor in December, and William was recalled to active duty in January. He served in Africa and Europe as part of the Military Police, traveling as a guard for German prisoners. He rose to the rank of staff sergeant.

The oldest Townsend brother, Halsey, was forty, married and living in Fort Hunter when inducted in 1942. Halsey worked for the Delaware & Hudson Railroad in Delanson. As a corporal in the army, he was a signalman and trainmaster in Tehran on the Trans-Iranian Railroad, which helped supply Russia.

Albert attained the rank of corporal with an armored division in France, Germany and Central Europe. He was badly burned in combat, requiring extensive hospital treatment.

Hubert also earned the rank of corporal. He served in France and Germany as a company clerk. Albert and Hubert met up when they were overseas.

Louis Junior earned the rank of technician third grade or staff sergeant serving in the jungles of New Guinea, fighting the Japanese in a hot and rainy climate. He also took part in the invasion of the Philippines. He worked on military vehicles in his three years overseas and was the last of the brothers to come home in 1946.

The brother-in-law who served in the army was William Kosboth, a medical corpsman in Europe. Kosboth had married one of the Townsend daughters, Marian Ethel. He was part of the Normandy invasion and soldiered on in France and Germany. Back home, Kosboth operated Fendly's Gas Station in Fort Johnson, started by his stepfather.

In civilian life, Louis Townsend Jr. worked at that gas station, American Locomotive, Mohasco and, for many years, at St. Mary's Hospital, retiring in 1987.

One Townsend son, Ray, did not serve in the military because of heart trouble. Another Townsend daughter, Edith, was the wife of popular Amsterdam police officer Andy Nelson.

When all the Townsends and Kosboth had come back from the war in February 1946, a reunion was held at the home of their sister Jeanette, who had married Fred Newbold of Tribes Hill.

The newspaper account stated, "It is pointed out that six members from one family survived several important phases of World War II in all parts of the world, three of the sons making a complete trip around the world."

Sergeant Watroba

Chester A. Watroba spent much of his life as a letter carrier and family man living on Austin Street in Amsterdam. Watroba also served in the U.S. Marines for nine years, including numerous bloody campaigns on Pacific Islands in World War II.

Watroba was promoted to sergeant with the First Marine Division and was a recipient of the Purple Heart. He had been promoted to corporal for actions on the enemy-held island of New Britain in the early morning of December 30, 1943.

According to a Marine Corps memo, Watroba

> *engaged the enemy in a fierce hand to hand combat preventing the enemy from taking our positions. After his machine gun had been bayoneted through the water jacket by the enemy, he assisted in clearing out the enemy by rifle fire and grenades. Though wounded in the face and arm and without regard for his feelings and safety, he gave battle to the enemy until the battle was over.*

Watroba also fought on Peleliu, Palau Islands, Okinawa, Shima, Ryukyu and Cape Gloucester. On Cape Gloucester, he was wounded while recapturing a heavy machine gun position overrun by the enemy.

Watroba and Regina Califano were married in 1948. He retired from the postal service because of a disability in 1975. Regina Watroba died in 1991, and Chester Watroba died in 1996 at age seventy-four. Daughter Sharon Watroba Burns of New York City provided information on her father. The marine was also survived by his son John of Amsterdam and daughter Arlene Perrault of Houston.

Online Memorial

John A. Haas has found an Internet honor roll of Americans based in Britain who were killed in action in World War II. The honor roll is also an actual book at the American Memorial Chapel at St. Paul's Cathedral in London, a part of the cathedral bombed during a German air raid and then rebuilt after the war. The chapel was paid for by the British people, and the book containing twenty-eight thousand American names was presented by General Dwight Eisenhower in 1951.

The book is reproduced online at http://www.stpauls.co.uk/Cathedral-History/The-Chapels/American-Memorial-Chapel.

Haas wrote, "I found my Uncle John L. Haas listed. I thought some of your readers might be interested in this fine memorial."

Technical Sergeant Haas of 87 Pawling Street in Hagaman was twenty-nine when he died on September 29, 1943, after going down with his plane over Germany. Sergeant Haas was a gunner on an American bomber. Before being inducted into the army, he had worked at Mohawk Carpet Mills.

Sergeant Haas was survived by his wife, Pearl. His parents were Amsterdam Eighth Ward alderman John L. Haas, Sr. and his wife, Blanche. He also left his brother Edison, who served in the army in India. Edison was the father of John A. Haas.

The family operated an auto repair garage on Lyon Street and Haas Variety Store, a popular teen hangout with a soda fountain, on Lindsay Street in Amsterdam's Rockton section during the 1950s.

HONOR ROLL

Amsterdam attorney Robert N. Going has written a remarkable book, *Honor Roll: The World War II Dead of Amsterdam, N.Y.* Using online newspaper archives, museum collections and personal diaries, Going provides information on 176 men from the Amsterdam area who died during and right after the war.

The first was William E. Hasenfuss Jr., from a family of nine children on Northampton Road. Hasenfuss had flown airplanes at an air field in Perth before enlisting in 1939. He died at Hickham Air Field in Hawaii in the Japanese attack on Pearl Harbor.

Going calls 1943 the "year of the plane crash." Among those who died that year in plane crashes was Lieutenant Donald Wemple, who grew up in Gloversville but married an Amsterdam girl, Doris Johnson. A football star, Wemple played professionally for the old Brooklyn Dodgers of the National Football League. Wemple's transport caught fire flying from India to China, and he tried to bring it home on one engine. He survived long enough to talk with a chaplain, who wrote to Wemple's widow.

Members of Amsterdam's National Guard Company G were among the three thousand Americans who died fighting Japanese human wave attacks

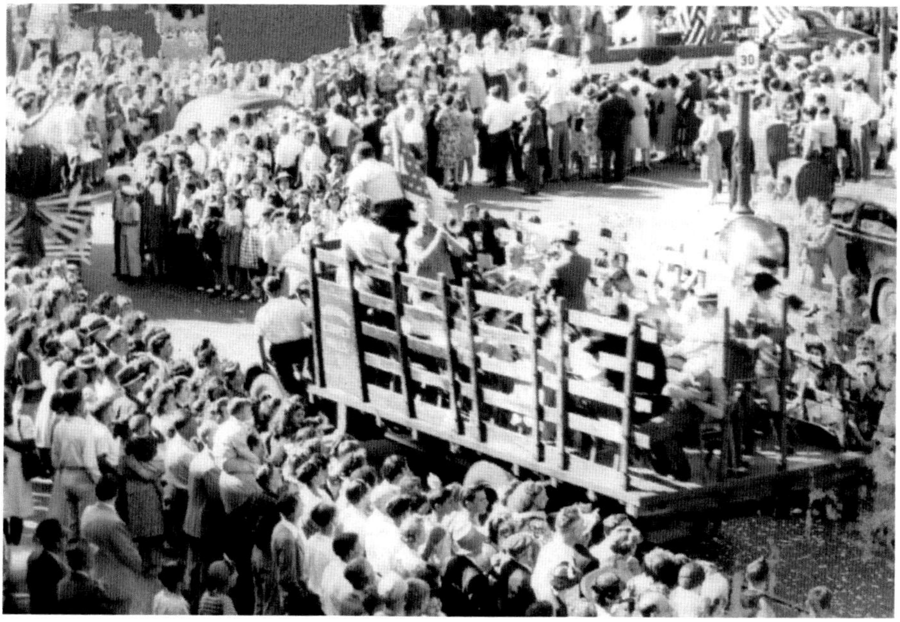

The Mohawk Mills Band on August 15, 1945, at a victory parade at Market and Main Streets in Amsterdam. *Walter Elwood Museum.*

on Saipan in 1944. Among the Saipan casualties were Sergeant Michael Makarowsky, Staff Sergeant Peter J. Sanzen, Private First Class Paul P. Sierota, Sergeant Edward R. Golenbiewski, Private First Class Daniel F. Slusarz and Captain Clinton F. Smith.

Private Walter Slavek had worked at Bigelow Sanford until joining the army in 1938. Captured in the Philippines, he survived the atrocities of Japanese prisoner of war camps and was in a cargo ship with seventeen hundred other prisoners bound for Japan in 1944. The ship was torpedoed by an American submarine. Slavek did not survive.

Among those killed in Normandy in 1944 were Private Frank J. Sirchia, Private First Class Thomas E. Cronin and Staff Sergeant George E. Brown. Private First Class Edward Popielarz went ashore on D-Day and was killed in October 1944 in France. In Amsterdam, he was known for raising homing pigeons.

Private Norman F. Briskie of Hagaman was nineteen when he was killed on January 5, 1945, in the Battle of the Bulge. Briskie's death was caused by the explosion of an artillery shell after his unit had fought the Germans in heavy snow to seize an important road.

The last Amsterdam casualty was Seaman Orlie Charles Thomas, who died in Brooklyn Naval Hospital on November 23, 1945. He had served aboard the battleship USS *Mississippi* in the Pacific.

Presumed Dead

An Amsterdam man presumed dead during World War II survived the war and lived until 2003. Going listed the death of Private First Class Anthony "Doc" Kosiba of 39 McCleary Avenue in *Honor Roll*.

Inducted in 1943, Kosiba arrived in England in the summer of 1944. He fought in France, Belgium and Germany. Kosiba's wife, Olga, received a telegram from the War Department that her husband was killed in action on German soil on October 6, 1944. His age was thirty-five. The *Recorder* printed Kosiba's obituary, and a funeral Mass was held.

After publication of his book, Going learned from family members that some days after the funeral, Olga Kosiba received a letter from her husband.

"It took a good deal of tear-wiping before she finally noticed the date on the letter," Going said. "It was after the date of the telegram announcing his death."

Going said that Kosiba had been wounded so badly that initially he was thought to be dead.

> *Doubtless his dog tags were gathered up and it was only later when they came back for the body that someone realized he was alive.*
>
> *After spending some time in Army hospitals, he came home to Olga and Amsterdam and lived a long and fruitful life.*

Kosiba earned the Purple Heart, Bronze Star and European Campaign medals. After the war, he returned to his job at the Fitzgerald Bottling Company in Amsterdam. He was a production manager for the Fitzgerald and PepsiCola companies until his retirement.

Olga Kosiba, who had worked for Mohasco, died in 1998. Anthony Kosiba died on March 6, 2003, at age ninety-four. The couple had no children.

USS *AMSTERDAM*

A light cruiser named for Amsterdam, New York, earned a battle star in 1945 for its role in the war against Japan. The navy began naming cruisers for American cities in the 1880s. President Franklin D. Roosevelt had chosen the name Amsterdam for a navy light cruiser in 1940, according to the U.S. Naval Historical Center in Washington. However, that warship was converted to an aircraft carrier and was launched in 1942 as the USS *Independence*.

Work began on what finally would become the USS *Amsterdam* in 1943 at the shipyard in Newport News, Virginia. A light cruiser is a warship that is not as large as a regular cruiser but is larger than a destroyer. There has been speculation that Amsterdam was granted the honor of having a cruiser named for it because of the work done for the war effort by the city's carpet mills and the close ties between the city's mayor, Arthur Carter, and President Roosevelt.

The *Amsterdam* was commissioned in January 1945. In addition to its guns, the two-toned, Cleveland-class light cruiser carried two Curtiss Seahawk floatplanes.

The *Amsterdam* class had increased range and better armament than earlier ships. The navy proposed building thirty-nine of these vessels, but only twenty-seven were built. The Amsterdam was 610 feet long and weighed ten thousand tons, and its top speed was 31.5 knots. It was the last cruiser of its class to see action in the war.

The *Amsterdam* had a crew of over fourteen hundred officers and enlisted men. The captain was Andrew P. Lawton. Among the crew was Steve Fitz from Schenectady, who went on to be a radio talk show host in Upstate New York and who currently does commentary for Amsterdam radio station WVTL-FM. Fitz was given a choice of three ships when leaving boot camp in 1945 and chose the *Amsterdam* because the name reminded him of home.

Local Gold Star mother Frieda Hasenfuss was the sponsor of the ship and spoke when the *Amsterdam* was commissioned in Virginia. Her son, army staff sergeant William Hasenfuss Jr., had died at Pearl Harbor, the city's first casualty of the war.

"About 55 percent of the crew was right out of boot camp," Fitz said. "There was a decent amount of old salts who knew their way around ships."

After shakedown cruises in Chesapeake Bay and the Caribbean, the *Amsterdam* sailed through the Panama Canal into the Pacific Ocean. The *Amsterdam* never crossed the equator, usually an occasion for something like a fraternity hazing for greenhorn sailors. However, the ship did cross the International Date Line, and veteran crew members convinced the captain to have two days of frivolity at the expense of the new recruits in mid-June. Soon, the ship reached Leyte in the Philippines for service with the Third Fleet.

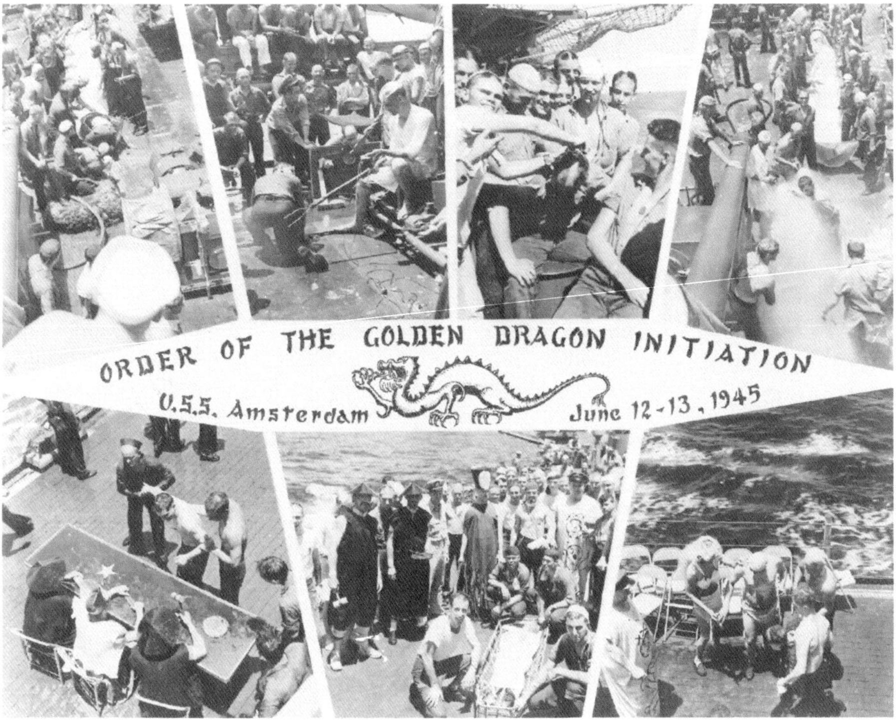

When the USS *Amsterdam* crossed the International Date Line in 1945, crew members celebrated. *Steve Fitz.*

A seaman first class, Fitz operated radar that guided antiaircraft guns. The *Amsterdam* protected aircraft carriers that sent planes to bomb Japan in July 1945. Among the cities attacked by these planes were Tokyo, Kure, Kobe and Osaka. The *Amsterdam* never fired its guns at the enemy; any Japanese resistance was held off by destroyers miles away.

"Ships would send bombers to Japan every day," Fitz said. "All of us were happy when they dropped the nuclear bombs. We knew we would be part of an invasion of Japan, and there would be a great loss of life."

When the Japanese capitulated, the *Amsterdam* was stationed off the coast of Honshu to guard against possible Japanese attacks. Fitz said one admiral told the sailors that the Japanese had surrendered, but if you see any Japanese aircraft, shoot them down in a friendly way.

The *Amsterdam* was part of the fleet in Tokyo Bay for surrender ceremonies that took place on the USS *Missouri*. Fitz could see General Macarthur and Japanese officials on the *Missouri* through his range finder.

After shore leave in Japan, the *Amsterdam* sailed back toward America, picking up Seabees in Guam. The passengers brought with them an outbreak of dysentery. They also brought a different perspective on the war to the *Amsterdam*'s sailors.

"We had a laundry, hot food, a ship's newspaper [*News of the Cruise*] and ice cream almost every day," Fitz said. "As we were traveling back to America, one of the crew in line for dinner shouted out there was no ice cream today. One of the Seabees said, 'Isn't that a shame. We haven't seen ice cream in two years!'"

The *Amsterdam* was the first large ship to go up the Columbia River to Portland, Oregon, in October 1945 to discharge its passengers and take part in Navy Day. The vessel then sailed to San Francisco, and the crew painted it.

The sailors were honorably discharged. The *Amsterdam* was decommissioned in 1947 and stored in San Francisco. The vessel was sold to a scrap yard in Terminal Island, California, in 1972.

Fitz attended a reunion held in Amsterdam some years ago and found it a very emotional experience. "There is bonding when you are stuck in a place like that," he said. "What it did was it taught us that you've got do what you're told and when you're told. It made men out of a lot of boys."

Fitz said that some Amsterdam politicians were reluctant to let USS *Amsterdam* veterans stage their reunion and parade, fearing they might get out of hand. "We were coming with our wives," Fitz said. The reunion took place without incident. Current city officials are working with the veterans of the USS *Amsterdam* in hopes that they will come back for at least one more reunion.

USS Lansing

According to the *Dictionary of American Fighting Ships*, the destroyer escort USS *Lansing* was named for Amsterdam native William Henry Lansing.

Lansing was born in 1914, enlisted in the navy in 1934 and became a pilot. He was killed by enemy fire during a dive-bombing and strafing attack on Japanese shipping in Kiska Harbor in the Aleutian campaign in 1942.

Sponsored by Lansing's widow, Alberta, the USS *Lansing* was commissioned in 1943. The destroyer escort accompanied eight convoys from America to North African ports starting in 1944. In June 1945, the *Lansing* was on its way to Pearl Harbor when news came of the Japanese surrender. The vessel became a Coast Guard ship in 1952 and reverted to the navy in 1956. The *Lansing* was scrapped in 1974.

The Museum and the Library

Walter Elwood and His Museum

Walter Elwood was a character. When he visited Amsterdam's schools, he walked because he didn't drive a car. He had a tall, robust but ungainly frame and a deep, gravelly voice. An educator, he was well loved by a generation of students. He was a world traveler, a collector and a conservationist. He wrote two novels and collaborated for a year with lyricist Oscar Hammerstein II.

Elwood had a "fund of knowledge," said retired Amsterdam library supervisor and educator Evelyn Riccio, adding that Elwood "liked nothing more than to talk about his travels, birds and seashells."

The Walter Elwood Museum is his legacy. Since 2009, the museum has been located at Guy Park Manor, built as a colonial home along the Mohawk River for members of the Johnson family.

Born in 1886 in the town of Florida, Walter Elwood was the son of Emory Elwood and Catherine Langenfelter. He graduated from Amsterdam High in 1904, earned a bachelor's degree at Cornell and went to the Philippines for four years to instruct teachers in that new American possession.

He wrote a novel called *Guimo* about a young Filipino man. According to the dust jacket, "With *Guimo* the veneer of civilization is thin—the red blood and the rich soul come all the closer to the surface." A second Elwood novel dealt with the Erie Canal and Port Jackson, the old name for Amsterdam's South Side. *Those Terrible Teenenfelters* was published after his death.

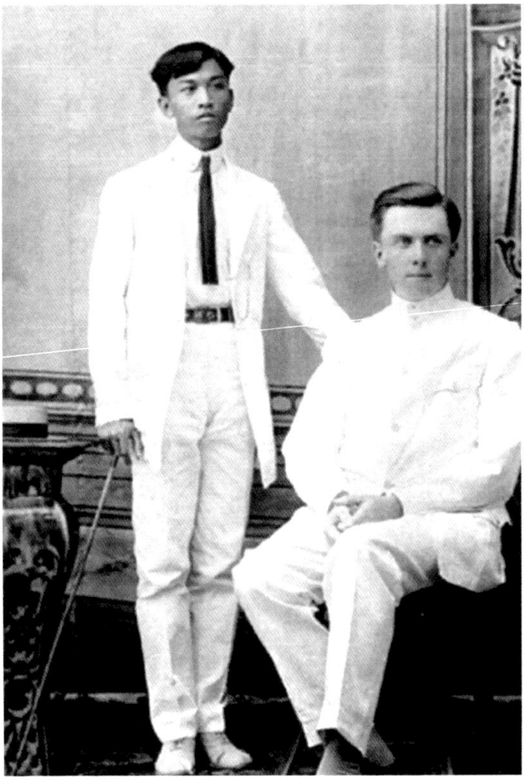

A Filipino student and Walter Elwood. *Walter Elwood Museum.*

When Elwood returned from the Philippines in 1912, he became principal of a school in New Market, New Jersey. In 1916, he volunteered to serve in France with the Red Cross in World War I. After the war, he spent a year in New York City as a playwright and author's assistant to Oscar Hammerstein II.

Elwood returned to Montgomery County and was superintendent of the county educational district. He began the county's 4-H Clubs. He taught at Guy Park Avenue School and the junior high in Amsterdam. He was one of the organizers of the city's Sassafrass Hollow bird sanctuary in 1931 and president of the Sassafras Bird Club.

In 1938, he began his Amsterdam Public School Museum, stocking six large rooms in the old Fifth Ward School on Perkins Street on the South Side with ten thousand items, many from his own collections. That building is gone now, and housing has been built in that location.

"I saw a small museum in Schenectady," Elwood told the *Recorder*, "and felt that what was good for Schenectady children was also good for those in Amsterdam. Now we have a better museum than the one in Schenectady."

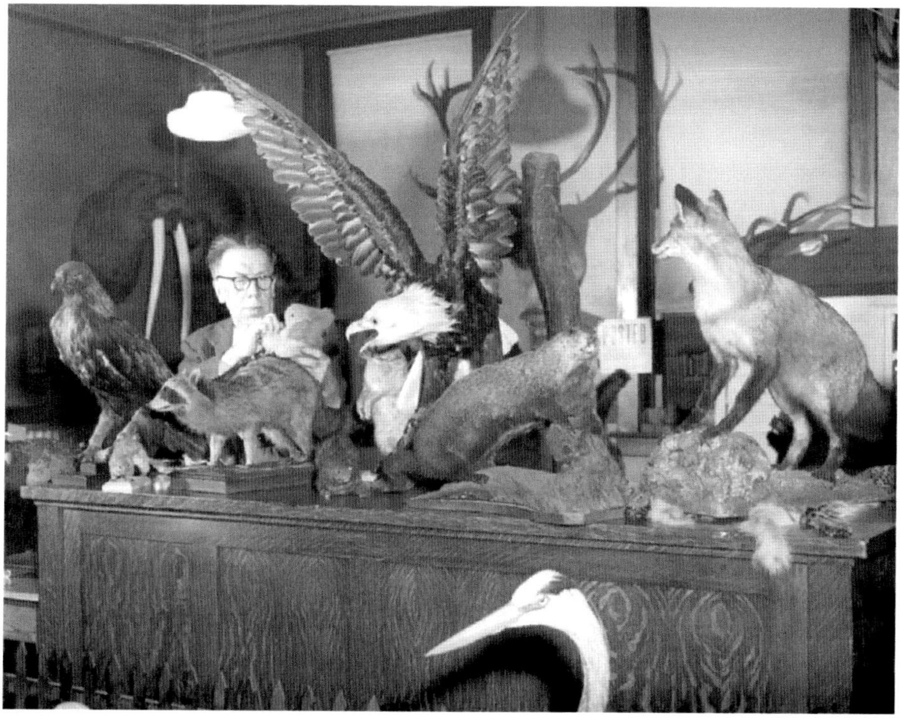

Walter Elwood and friends at his Amsterdam museum. *Walter Elwood Museum.*

There were international, early American, animal, bird and geology rooms in the South Side museum. The international collection included robes from Africa, a bamboo pillow from China and sleeping mats from the Philippines. An elephant's foot was popular. Elwood used to have young children stand inside the foot to emphasize the elephant's size.

Elwood supervised the city's Victory Gardens in World War II, headed the county SPCA for sixteen years and helped rewrite the state's science and social studies syllabus in 1951 to include information on conservation.

His first wife died early on. In 1926, he married her sister, Anna Bevillard Mack from Chicago. Anna survived him; they had no children. Walter Elwood died on April 28, 1955. Ill health had led to his resignation from the school system three months earlier.

Amanda Powell, one of Elwood's assistants (the other was Nellie Brannigan), kept the museum going until 1960. The museum collection was moved from the South Side to the former Guy Park Avenue School across the river, and the museum opened there in 1968. Through the years that followed, whatever artifacts came through the door were seldom refused.

The late Mary Margaret Gage was museum director for many years. Ann Thane later held that post but left when she was elected Amsterdam mayor in 2007. Since then, Ann Peconie has been museum executive director.

Ties were severed with the school district in 2009, and the museum left its former school location on Guy Park Avenue and moved to Guy Park Manor, a state-owned building. Today, the museum is operated by a nonprofit organization called the Walter Elwood Museum of the Mohawk Valley.

Amsterdam Free Library

Carved in stone over the entrance to the Amsterdam Free Library at 28 Church Street are the words "Open to All."

Generations of Amsterdamians are familiar with the insides of the stately old building with its oak woodwork, large reading tables and second-floor children's section. The present library opened in 1903. A wing at the rear of the building was added in 1980.

The first organized book collection in the city was the Amsterdam Union Library, founded in 1805 and operated one day a week from the home of the librarian. The Amsterdam Literary Association was formed in the 1840s to promote literature, and the association lasted at least until 1860.

Speakers were invited to winter sessions, but the bylaws stipulated that speakers be paid no more than travel expenses. When there was no speaker, topics were debated, such as "Is the motto, Our Country Right or Wrong, consistent with true patriotism?"

On January 14, 1848, an unknown topic was discussed with "a good deal of irregular conversation between members—whereupon on or about the hour of ten and without any motion being put, the meeting broke in a row." At the next meeting, the minutes were altered by changing "row" to "disorder."

In 1891, prominent citizens led by two physicians, William H. Robb and Samuel H. French, founded the Amsterdam Library Association. That library was located on East Main Street, west of Church Street. It was not a free library—members paid a subscription fee of one dollar a year.

In 1895, the facility became a free library after a fundraising campaign organized by women in the community and sponsored by the *Daily Democrat* newspaper, a forerunner of the *Recorder*. A special women's edition of the newspaper sold ten thousand copies and raised $1,500.

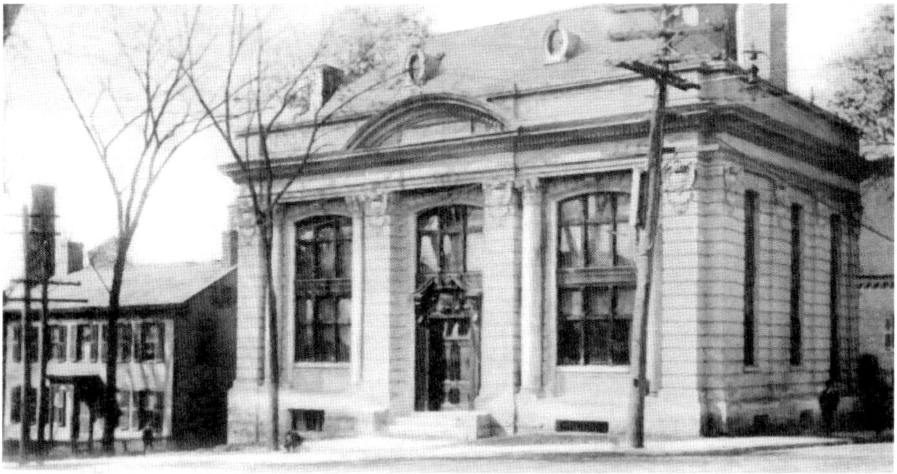

Amsterdam Free Library, constructed in 1903. *Gerald B. Snyder.*

The Library Association became the Amsterdam Free Library in 1902 after a donation of $25,000 from philanthropist and industrialist Andrew Carnegie, who was solicited by Dr. French. Carnegie agreed to put up the money to construct the building in exchange for the city's pledge for ongoing financial support.

Historian Hugh Donlon wrote that city aldermen were hesitant about the cost of ongoing library maintenance but went along with the proposal after a meeting at Alderman Frank Parmentier's saloon on Railroad Street.

At the library's 1903 cornerstone ceremony, Dr. French paid tribute to the city's growing industrial importance: "The whir of spindle and wheel will penetrate even the rooms set apart to reading and meditation, a constant reminder of the fact that thought and action must be inseparable. The toiler, not the idler is the one for whom libraries are founded."

Through the years, natives of the city, including movie actor Kirk Douglas, have remembered the library with donations. Douglas honored his friend Sonya Jacobsen Seigel with a library gift.

The library today offers much more than books. Its computer stations are patronized by young people doing homework and older people getting jobs or pursuing other interests. Computer literacy classes are popular, as are community-wide programs such as Amsterdam Reads.

The library has continued to receive city funds. The Friends of the Amsterdam Free Library also raises money for the institution and is seeking new members. Membership forms are available at the library or online.

Further Reading on Mohawk Valley History

Beers, Frederick W. *History of Montgomery and Fulton Counties*. New York: F.W. Beers & Co., 1878.

Cudmore, Bob. *You Can't Go Wrong: Stories from Nero, New York and other Tales*. Glenville, NY: Nero Publishing, 2000.

Dauria, Susan R. *Deindustrialization and the Construction of History and Ethnic Identity: The Case of Amsterdam, New York*. PhD diss., University at Albany, 1999.

Donlon, Hugh P. *Annals of a Mill Town: Amsterdam, New York*. Schenectady, NY: Donlon Associates, 1980.

———. *Outlines of History: Montgomery County*. Amsterdam, NY, 1973.

Douglas, Kirk. *The Ragman's Son: An Autobiography*. New York: Simon and Schuster, 1988.

Dunn, Russell. *Adventures Around the Great Sacandaga Lake*. Utica, NY: Nicholas K. Burns Publishing, 2002.

Farquhar, Kelly Yacobucci. *Montgomery County: Images of America*. Charleston, SC: Arcadia, 2004.

Farquhar, Kelly Yacobucci, and Scott G. Haefner. *Amsterdam: Images of America*. Charleston, SC: Arcadia, 2006.

Going, Robert N. *Honor Roll: The World War II Dead of Amsterdam, N.Y.* Amsterdam, NY: George Street Press, 2010.

Golab, Adam. *The Mighty and Awesome Chuctanunda Creeks Runs Through a Limestone City*. N.p., 1999.

Greene, Nelson. *History of the Mohawk Valley: Gateway to the West 1614–1925.* Chicago: S.J. Clarke Publishing Co., 1925.

Hayes, W. Parker, Jr. *Drawn Home: Fritz Vogt's Rural America*. Cooperstown: New York State Historical Association, 2002.
Hildebrandt, Louis. *Riders Up*. N.p.: Sierra Solutions ADK, 2003.
Hildebrandt, Louis, Jr. *Hurricana: Thoroughbred Dynasty, Amsterdam Landmark*. Troy, NY: Troy Bookmakers, 2009.
Huey, Lois M., and Bonnie Pulis. *Molly Brant: A Legacy of Her Own*. Youngstown, NY: Old Fort Niagara Association, 1997.
Keesler, Paul M. *Mohawk: Discovering the Valley of the Crystals*. Utica, NY: North Country Books, 2009.
Larner, Paul K. *Our Railroad: The History of the Fonda, Johnstown & Gloversville Railroad (1867–1893)*. Bloomington, IN: Author House, 2009.
McMartin, Barbara, and W. Alec Reid. *The Glove Cities: How a People and Their Craft Built Two Cities*. Caroga, NY: Lakeview Press, 1999.
Murphy, Jacqueline Daly. *St. Mary's Parish: A History*. Amsterdam, NY: St. Mary's Church, 2004.
Pacelli, Tony. *Past and Present: Nostalgia, Amsterdam and Surrounding Communities*. Amsterdam, NY: The Recorder, 1987.
Pietrusza, David. *Baseball's Canadian-American League*. N.p.: McFarland & Co., 2005.
Reid, W. Max. *The Mohawk Valley: Its Legends and Its History*. New York: G.P. Putnam, 1901.
Robb, Alex M. *The Sanfords of Amsterdam*. New York: William-Frederick Press, 1969.
Simms, Jeptha R. *The Frontiersman of New York*. N.p., 1883.
———. *History of Schoharie County and Border Wars of New York*. Albany, NY, 1845.
———. *The Trappers of New York*. N.p., 1850.
Skivington, Deborah J. *General George Washington in the Mohawk Valley: Summer, 1783*. Fort Plain, NY: Fort Plain Museum, 2002.
Snyder, Gerald R., and Robert von Hasseln. *Amsterdam, Postcard History Series*. Charleston, SC: Arcadia, 2010.
Strobeck, Katherine M. *Mohawk Valley Happenings*. Fort Johnson, NY: Montgomery County Historical Society, 1990.
———. *Port Jackson: An Erie Canal Village*. Port Jackson, NY: Port Jackson Publishing Co., 1989.
Todd, Nancy L. *New York's Historic Armories*. Albany, NY: SUNY Press, 2006.
Tralka, George A. *Diary of a Replacement Soldier*. N.p.: Xlibris, 2011.

Online Information

Tom Tryniski maintains a database of many newspapers in New York State. http://www.fultonhistory.com/Fulton.html.

Frank Yunker maintains a database with many of Bob Cudmore's *Daily Gazette* columns, plus other information. www.mohawkvalleyweb.com.

Peter Sefton has a website on lost Upstate New York landmarks. www.lostlandmarks.org.

Documentaries

Bannon, Colin. *True Stories from Rug City*. Syracuse, NY: Syracuse University, 2007.

Dunn, Steve, and Bob Cudmore. *Historic Views of the Carpet City: Amsterdam, N.Y.* WMHT, 2000.

Durfee, Joanne. *Our Town Amsterdam*. WMHT, 2010. www.wmht.org.

Rombout, Rob, and Rogier van Eck. *Amsterdam Stories USA*. Belgian Cultural Board [in production].

About the Author

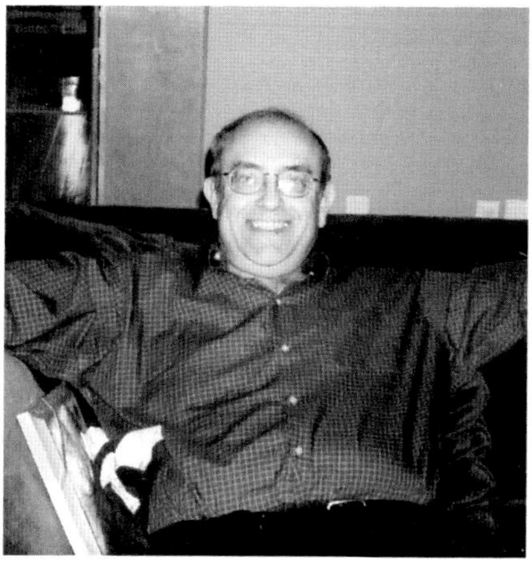

Bob Cudmore is a native of Amsterdam, New York, who has written a regular column on Mohawk Valley history for the *Daily Gazette* newspaper for over a decade. He and Steve Dunn co-produced a ninety-minute WMHT-TV documentary about Amsterdam history—*Carpet City*—in 2000. That same year, Cudmore published the book *You Can't Go Wrong: Stories from Nero, N.Y. and Other Tales*, a satirical look at Upstate life.

A radio and television talk show host, Cudmore most recently hosted the morning show on Lite 104.7/1570 AM WVTL radio in Amsterdam. From 1980 to 1993, he hosted the nightly *Contact* talk show on WGY radio in Albany.

An adjunct instructor in media at Albany's College of St. Rose, Cudmore worked in public relations for the State University of New York System Administration from 1993 to 2001. He has a master's and a bachelor's in English from Boston University. He lives in Glenville and has two children—Bob Cudmore Jr. of Baltimore, Maryland, and Kathleen R. Bokan of West Charlton, New York.

Visit us at

www.historypress.net

www.bobcudmore.com